HEALING beyond COUNSELING

A Handbook to Healing

GARY HEESE

WESTBOW
PRESS®
A DIVISION OF THOMAS NELSON
& ZONDERVAN

Copyright © 2016 Gary Heese.

All rights reserved. No part of this book may be used or reproduced by any means, graphic, electronic, or mechanical, including photocopying, recording, taping or by any information storage retrieval system without the written permission of the author except in the case of brief quotations embodied in critical articles and reviews.

This book is a work of non-fiction. Unless otherwise noted, the author and the publisher make no explicit guarantees as to the accuracy of the information contained in this book and in some cases, names of people and places have been altered to protect their privacy.

Unless otherwise noted, all Scripture quotations are taken from the *New King James Version* (NKJV), copyright 1982 by Thomas Nelson, Inc. Used by permission. All rights reserved.

Scripture quotations marked (KJV) are from the King
James Version of the Bible (public domain).

Scripture quotations marked (LB) are from *The Living Bible* copyright 1971 by Tyndale House Foundation. Used by permission of Tyndale House Publishers Inc., Carol Stream, Illinois 60188. All rights reserved.

Scripture quotations marked (NASB) are taken from the *New American Standard Bible*, copyright 1960, 1962, 1963, 1971, 1972, 1973, 1975, 1977 by The Lockman Foundation. Used by permission. All rights reserved.

Scripture quotations marked (NIV) are from the *Holy Bible, New International Version* (NIV), copyright 1973, 1978, 1984, 2011 Biblica, Inc. Used by permission. All rights reserved.

Scripture quotations marked (NLT) are taken from the *Holy Bible, New Living Translation*, copyright 1996. Used by permission of Tyndale House Publishers, Inc., Wheaton, IL 60189 USA. Used by permission. All rights reserved.

All *italics* shown in Scripture quotations represent the author's added emphasis.

WestBow Press books may be ordered through booksellers or by contacting:

WestBow Press
A Division of Thomas Nelson & Zondervan
1663 Liberty Drive
Bloomington, IN 47403
www.westbowpress.com
1 (866) 928-1240

Because of the dynamic nature of the Internet, any web addresses or links contained in this book may have changed since publication and may no longer be valid. The views expressed in this work are solely those of the author and do not necessarily reflect the views of the publisher, and the publisher hereby disclaims any responsibility for them.

Any people depicted in stock imagery provided by Thinkstock are models, and such images are being used for illustrative purposes only.
Certain stock imagery © Thinkstock.

ISBN: 978-1-5127-3903-9 (sc)
ISBN: 978-1-5127-3904-6 (hc)
ISBN: 978-1-5127-3902-2 (e)

Library of Congress Control Number: 2016906613

Print information available on the last page.

WestBow Press rev. date: 5/10/2016

Contents

Foreword ix
Our Story xi

1. **Getting Started** 1
2. **Spiritual Bondage** 11
   Unforgiveness 13
   Relinquishment 33
   Idolatry 46
   Condemnation 48
   Inner Vows and Pledges 49
   Bitter Root Judgments 52
   Curses 54
   The Occult and False Religions 59
   Soul Ties 67
   Inappropriate Authority 72
   Dishonor and Shame 74
   Self-Pity 79
   Generational or Hereditary Sins 85
   National or Ethnic Bondages 87
   Ministry Preparation 90
3. **The Road to Redemption** 93
4. **The Helper Skills** 98
   Listening 98

	Identify the Bondages	109
	Physical Touch	109
	Prayer	112
	Compassion	115
	Cultural Sensitivity	117
	Confrontation	118
	Control	119
	Next Steps	121
5.	**Ministry Models**	**123**
	Help Them Forgive	128
	Rejection	132
	Abandonment	136
	Relationship Conflict	137
	Control	146
	Adult Child of Alcoholics	148
	Adult Children of Divorce	151
	Miscarriage or Stillbirth	154
	Abortion	155
	Breaking Soul Ties	158
	Inappropriate Authority	161
	Sexual Abuse, Molestation, or Incest	162
	Domestic Violence	167
	Unwed or Single Mothers	171
	Addictions	174
	Identificational Repentance	178
	Performance Orientation	180
	Suicide	182
	Father/Mother Heart Ministry	183
	Ministry Preparation	187
	Prayer Models	189

6. **Rebuilding, Part I** 194
    Renewing Your Mind 195
7. **Rebuilding, Part II** 207
    I Am Scriptures 215
    "The Dirty Dozen" 223
    Names of God 224

Resources for Rebuilding 227

Foreword

This work that Gary has produced brings joy to my heart. He has drawn from many of our resource teachers in the Biblical Counseling Schools of the College, along with others, as well as many years of life and ministry experience to compile these important truths.

His presentation on the helper–seeker relationship highlights the powerful biblical dynamic that releases warmth, empathy, respect, and the love that replaces fear with trust and transparency.

Active listening principles and practice are seen to be relation-saving and -restoring elements that lay the foundation for deeper ministry.

He also examines an extensive list of current conditions from a biblical standpoint, highlighting the principles and skills to practice better management of them.

Above all, the Holy Spirit is acknowledged as the one whose gifts and power are essential for healing, deliverance, and the making of a disciple.

The rebuilding process is explained and elaborated in the latter chapters of the book. This process is crucially important.

A failure to follow up on ministry often results in losing ground gained by the seeker.

I highly recommend this excellent work to all who have a desire to move in a biblical counseling ministry.

Bless you, Gary, as you continue to multiply wonderful counselors for the kingdom.

Dr. Bruce Thompson,
Foundational Dean, College of Counseling and Health Care, University of the Nations, Kailua Kona Campus, Hawaii

Our Story

Thousands of men and women over the decades have been moved by the Spirit of God to step out in faith for the purpose of extending His kingdom on earth. This step of faith is usually propelled by an unmistakable urge from the Holy Spirit. This process is no different than it was two thousand years ago when ordinary people were challenged to do the unthinkable: Jesus asked the first disciples to quit their jobs, leave their homes, and follow Him. In return, the Lord would make them "fishers of men." In this same way, my wife and I were also challenged. It seemed as though we were "drop-kicked" into this new journey with God—a journey with an itinerary that only He could have planned. We needed only to say yes. And the same way thousands before us have done, we needed only to take that first step.

My wife, Carla, and I were happily working in different ministries at our local church in Kansas City. We had participated in a few outreaches through the church and were excited about all we had experienced. Then one summer day in 1988 our mission pastor gave us the book *Is That Really You, God?* by Loren Cunningham. We started reading the book on a weekend, and by Monday we were no longer content with the ordinary or life as we knew it. I was in the construction business, and no longer could I be satisfied cutting long boards into short boards or remodeling bathrooms simply because they weren't the right color. I knew it was time my labor began reaping eternal benefits for the kingdom of God.

Many are the stories of men and women who were led to the mission field by a particular Scripture that jumped from the page or by a country that God had laid upon their hearts. I was not motivated by either. In fact, aside from my experience in construction, I had little to offer God. Then one day a line from Numbers 22:28 was brought to mind—"Then the Lord opened the mouth of the donkey"—and I concluded that if God could use a donkey, He could use me.

Loren Cunningham had founded a mission organization called Youth with a Mission (YWAM), and we wanted to be a part of what God was doing through this organization. We began the application process for our family, including our eighteen-year-old daughter, to attend training schools in YWAM. In September of 1988, Carla, our daughter Patty, and I headed to Hawaii, and our wonderful journey with the Lord had begun.

God placed us in the discipleship schools at YWAM, working with young adults. Most of the students attending the discipleship schools had a desire to pursue a career in ministry, but we found that very often these potential ministers needed to deal with pain from their own past before they could be effective in ministry themselves. Carla and I wanted to help those who were struggling with these wounds. While Carla was a natural with this kind of ministry, I did not possess either the skills or training to help them. We promptly enrolled in the Introduction to Biblical Counseling class at YWAM.

Carla and I were experiencing our own struggles at the time and were in marriage counseling ourselves. Our relationship had deteriorated to the point that we had the same feelings for each other that one might have toward a person you are passing in the grocery store ... in the frozen food section. The Counseling School not only taught us how to help others, but it was a place of healing in our own lives. As we continued to help in the Counseling and Discipleship Schools with YWAM over the next three years, we began to witness healing in other people's lives. And as is always the case in ministry, we received healing and blessing ourselves while helping others.

Shortly after we returned home to Kansas City in 1993, our pastor approached us with a need he had identified in the church. A woman had come to him with a situation that was becoming all too common: She had been a Christian for seventeen years, and after numerous altar calls, hours of praying, more hours of counseling, and several prescription medications, she was nearly void of hope. Finally she asked, "Isn't there any help for me?" Our pastor asked if we could help not only this woman but many others from similar life circumstances.

Because of his request, we began planning a ministry based on what we had experienced in YWAM. We met with our friends who had given us the book by Loren Cunningham (they had also served in YWAM) every week for about three months, and in the fall of 1994 the four of us offered the first course to our church, known as "Oaks of Righteousness." It was a twelve-week course, designed to benefit anyone who had wounds or regrets from their past. We used the materials and ministry models that we learned while serving in YWAM.

The class provided a safe environment that empowered the participants to break down the walls that had imprisoned them and allow Christ's healing power to set them free. By the third class, the enrollment was too many to facilitate in our home. I found myself telling those who completed the course to "go and tell no one."

This was no longer a Mom and Pop ministry; we had to begin training others. Since then, we have trained about 150 individuals in the Kansas City area and have multiplied to five other churches.

The program has grown so rapidly that our church has a waiting list of seekers who desire to experience God's healing through the class. Our church has also taken the class to maximum security prisons, where desperate men and women are experiencing the miracle of God's healing and are being set free from walls constructed of materials much stronger than man-made bricks. Hundreds of people have gone through a life-changing transition using the principles and ministry models described in this book.

Our Purpose

We have one goal with everything we do in the Inner Healing Ministry. We want to bring people a measure of healing in their lives, which in turn opens them to a greater revelation of who God is as their Father. When that happens, their identity is established; they know who they are, and they know their value. They learn to detach themselves from both the praise and the criticism of others, because they understand that God made them on purpose. As a result, they can begin to become who God created them specifically to be. Many who have been ministered to through "Oaks of Righteousness" are now in full-time ministry themselves.

The purpose of this book is to assist and train pastors and lay leaders in this style of ministry and to apply the redemption of the cross to every area of believers' lives, so they might become the persons God dreamed they could be when He fashioned them in the womb.

The Culture Trap

After spending five years in missions and watching people's lives transformed through this ministry, returning to my old life in the construction business became something like a slow death. I could sense the subtle force of our North American culture creeping back into our way of living. In the mission field, we depended on God to provide everything, even the basic necessities. We had no other option but to pray for our daily needs, wait on God, and believe. And like the Israelites in the desert receiving their daily manna, we saw miracle after miracle. With life in the States, when something wasn't happening, I could make it happen. If there was a special need, I knew where to go in order to meet that need.

We couldn't just leave behind all that God had taught us and equipped us to do, or we would lose it. We had to continue what He had begun. I needed to see the dead brought back to life again. This was not so much an identity crisis as a quality of life crisis. One way I could survive in this culture was to resume the healing ministry and see God at work in a tangible way once again. Besides, when we returned home after experiencing and learning what we did. I felt I was going to pop if I couldn't tell someone "the good news". Jesus really did come "that we might have life"!

The Center of Our Ministry

> The Spirit of the Lord God is upon Me,
> Because the Lord has anointed Me
> To preach good tidings to the poor;
> He has sent Me to *heal the brokenhearted,*

To proclaim liberty to the captives,
And the opening of the prison to those who are bound;
To proclaim the acceptable year of the Lord,
And the day of vengeance of our God;
To comfort all who mourn,
To console those who mourn in Zion,
To give them beauty for ashes,
The oil of joy for mourning,
The garment of praise for the spirit of heaviness;
That they may be called *oaks of righteousness*,
The planting of the Lord, that He may be glorified. (Isaiah 61:1–3)

Be Transformed

During this first year on the mission field, I came to realize that my belief system was not my own. I held opinions, prejudices, and judgments about individuals, people groups, and other things I knew nothing about. My way of thinking and my attitudes had been formed by cultural norms and the opinions of my authority figures, peers, or the media. Much of what I perceived as true could not stand when held to the light of truth in Scripture.

I grew up in a peaceful home. We had great relationship with each other and with extended family as well. So the dysfunction in our home was minor. However, when I got saved, there were a few opinions and beliefs that instantly changed. I had solid conviction about a few Christian values that are agreed upon and recognized throughout the Christian world, but after a few months in missions I realized that I had many more beliefs that needed to change as well.

It was going to require a determined decision for me to walk out of Egypt. The truth of Romans 12:2 became clear in my spirit: "Do not be conformed to this world, but *be transformed by the renewing of your mind*, that you may prove what is that good and acceptable and perfect will of God."

A key principle in this ministry is purposeful transformation by the renewing of our minds. It is our mission to see the captives set free, to witness the Holy Spirit's opening of blind eyes to see. We are about the business of binding up the brokenhearted and comforting those who mourn, and all this is done for the glory of God the Father.

CHAPTER 1

Getting Started

It seems, most of the time, when we are in pain, before seeking a healthy choice for solving or dealing with our struggles, we are naturally inclined to try a variety of mistaken choices to cope with our issues. Some of us try to cope by performing at work, getting married, having an affair, or getting divorced; we believe our comfort awaits in another relationship, another job, another house. Sometimes we cope with the pain through compulsive behaviors or addictions, and sometimes we become overwhelmed to the point that we sink into self-pity or depression.

Some of us take a positive step and attempt counseling, medications, or twelve-step groups. And these steps can be instrumental in beginning the process of inner healing. But many of us, either through the yearning of our own spirits to be complete, or the prompting of God's Holy Spirit, find ourselves at a fork in the road and finally understand that complete healing cannot be achieved by our own devices; we need God and the power of the cross. These are the ones who have "come to an end of themselves." And those who are desperate are those God can help the most.

Psychologist Carl Jung kept a bottle of champagne in the drawer of his desk. Anytime one of his patients came to his office with the news they'd lost their job, he quickly told them to sit down. He would pull the champagne out along with two glasses. After pouring a glass for the patient and for himself, he would say, "Let's celebrate. Something very good is going to happen for you now."

Jung, as a scientist, came to a very surprising conclusion. He once made the statement: "I do not have faith that there is a God … I know it." According to Jung, in all the hundreds of patients he treated, not one of them ever began to experience permanent healing until they acknowledged a need for God.

The Many Ways to Healing

It is usually the storms of life that cause those in need to reach out for help, and quite often the church is one of the last options they will pursue. Whatever mind-set a person in need comes with, we are happy to provide help. This book, we hope, will equip the church to provide what the seeker needs. This program is designed for spiritual and emotional healing. Depending on people's circumstances, they may have pursued any number of methods for healing: counseling, twelve-step programs, support groups, college classes, medication, or treatment facilities. Whatever the steps an individual may go through in their journey, any one of these—or a combination of them—may be needed and be an integral part of the healing process. However, the application of the spiritual aspect of healing is a necessary step for complete and permanent healing. Many fall short of being made whole, either because they aren't aware of their spiritual need or because they don't know what spiritual healing looks like. And the truth will always remain for anyone in need of healing, that "timing is everything."

One component of the human condition is that it's not until we are broken and desperate that we reach out to God. In truth, God will often allow us to experience heartbreak and loss in order to draw us toward the redemptive power of the cross. Indeed, our spiritual healing must always begin at the cross and applying that principle to our individual circumstance. When a seeker experiences the weight of burdens being lifted, either through the confession and forgiveness of their own sin or through forgiving another and releasing that pain they've been carrying for years, the seeker will desire even more freedom. And lo, the journey toward complete healing has begun.

When reflecting on all the different denominations, church movements, countries, and cultures we have ministered to, I am convinced the church is only scratching the surface in terms of applying the power of the cross to our lives. Too many Christians accept Jesus as their Savior and then simply wait for their own death or for Christ to return. Too many Christians are accepting mediocrity in their emotional lives, mistakenly believing that accepting pain and sorrow are what Jesus meant when He said that those who do not hate their own life are not His disciples. The church as a whole is effectively communicating the need for Christ, and miracles are surely happening. However, our program addresses how to apply the power of the cross to the hidden areas of our lives.

For many of us, what needs to take place will not be accomplished in three minutes at the altar after the Sunday service, and it will rarely take place in the setting of a small group. Inner healing requires brothers and sisters who are mature in their faith, working one on one, listening to each one's story, and walking with them in a time of ministry by praying, forgiving, releasing, and renouncing until they are free. This one-on-one commitment to assist in another person's healing may take multiple two-hour meetings and ministry times to accomplish freedom for one seeking help. What Jesus accomplished at the cross is magnificently more than what the majority of Christians are experiencing in their day-to-day lives. Notice I said two-hour meetings. I seldom help a person to a point of release before one-hour and forty minutes of ministry.

Offering Hope

The experience of most Christians who are in pain looks something like the following: they come to a place in their lives where the hurt causes them to reach out to someone they trust or someone they think can help. The seekers become transparent and begin to share deep heart issues. We calm them down and pray for them. We then offer to continue praying for them and maybe even suggest they seek counseling or another version of professional help.

But the church has much more to offer. The mandate given to the church in Isaiah 61:1–3 is to offer hope for the hurting, bind up the brokenhearted, and set the captives free. In order for the church to do this, we must train leaders in the ways of deep heart ministry. Referring someone who is in need of spiritual healing to a psychologist who does not apply the power of the cross will not help the seeker become whole. Similarly, a pastor who operates under the spiritual gifts of pastor, teacher, and evangelist can also be equipped with the tools necessary in deep heart ministry in order to help a member find freedom from emotional and spiritual bondage.

The various ministries and groups within the church provide much-needed healing and recovery for members at different stages of the healing process. Some groups receive individuals who are recently saved; others receive people who have been released from rehab facilities or directly from jail or those recently divorced or widowed; some receive people who are recently unemployed, those who are hungry, or even those who are homeless. Each group meets the person at different stages in their journey of healing and time of need. YWAM ministered to the nations by a slogan "going to the nations taking the two handed Gospel" the meaning being, (meet a person's felt need and present them the Gospel of Christ).

We offer a model of ministry that offers hope to those who remain in spiritual bondage to wounds from their past, wounds that continue to seep poison into their spirits and need to be expunged. This book offers several principles to apply in releasing prisoners from the walls and shackles of spiritual and emotional bondage.

The Seeker's Guide

If you are reading this book as a seeker, please consider the sources of hurts or bondages that may still be present in your life. There are many different sources of bondage; many you are probably aware of, but some perhaps not. Most of us begin with several of these areas to work on. Most of us will not be able to address every issue all at once. If you identify with this, please divide your issues into separate parts, and pray with a spiritually mature believer about what the Lord is revealing to you.

The process described in this book will reveal the roots of different spiritual bondages and identify the unresolved hurt or unconfessed sin in our lives. Once the bondage is identified, this book describes how to apply the redemption of the cross to be set free. The unresolved hurts in our lives directly affect how we function in all relationships. The pain from these hurts can have diverse effects, ranging from compulsive-addictive behaviors that cause us to act irrationally, to isolation and withdrawal from the outside world. When left unresolved, these hurts can affect how we function in a career, marriage, or family. The unwanted consequences of unresolved pain can affect our finances and even our physical or mental health.

Some of the sources of spiritual pain are listed below and are accompanied by biblical principles by which the Lord will bring healing and freedom from bondage.

Rejection

Rejection is the most common source of pain in our lives. The rejection may come through words of criticism or judgment or through verbal abuse of many sorts. But nonverbal communication can show strong signs of disapproval or rejection as well. Examples of nonverbal rejection are parents raising their eyebrows, shrugging their shoulders, or shaking their heads in disgust. Gestures like these can be just as rejecting as the words themselves. We are beginning to understand that even babies still in the womb can sense rejection.

Each of us reacts differently to the feeling of rejection, depending on our personality and temperament. Someone with a strong personality or a strong will, may react to rejection through rebellion. These people are, in essence, rejecting their rejection. They express through their actions that "I will reject you before you can reject me." Of course, most of the time this is happening unconsciously. This defense mechanism obviously affects our relationships as adults, because we continuously defend ourselves from further pain, which inhibits any kind of true intimacy with another person.

Someone with a more passive personality may have a broken will and live from a root of rejection. These people have a tendency to withdraw into themselves; they experience shame and depression, rejecting themselves and avoiding relationships. When these people experience life through the lens of rejection, they can feel a sense of hopelessness and become suicidal.

Rejection in the form of physical abandonment can also have serious and long-lasting effects on a child. When a parent abandons a child, that child feels the most extreme form of rejection. The child in this circumstance will most likely react one of two ways: abnormally clinging to the parent who is present, or expressing abnormal anger. As an adult, this person is very likely to become controlling or possessive in relationships.

With some people, rejection has taken root so deeply that they come to reject themselves. These people are susceptible to permanently taking on the role of the victim. People who have rejected themselves will often move somewhat aimlessly from one job to another. They will start a new job and perform well, but something will happen that causes them to fear yet another rejection or dismissal. Suddenly, they begin coming in late and not completing given tasks on time, and they manipulate themselves to the point where they are eventually fired. They are not aware of their motivation, but what they are doing is proving to everyone that they deserve rejection. They settle into the all-too-comfortable role of victim.

A more common but not easily recognized form of abandonment is emotional abandonment. A parent may be physically present—performing all the expected functions—but not present emotionally. Children of these parents often say things like "I know my dad loves me; he's just not very good at showing it."

All of these forms of rejection can cause us to believe lies about ourselves, such as "I am unworthy," "I am not lovable," "I don't measure up," or "I'm worthless."

False Prophets

Negative words spoken over us by others are equivalent to false prophets in our lives. A person in a position of authority, or even our peers, may have spoken words that are hurtful, critical, or negative. If we dwell on those words and take them into our spirit, they can become internalized and become a part of our inner being.

Judgments

Some statements judge us for being something we are not or exaggerate who we are. Examples of this would be a parent saying to the child, "You are worthless," or "You are just like your dad," or "You are stupid." Unfortunately, these judgments can last well into the child's adult years, thus perpetuating the destructive consequences. One scenario of this goes as follows: the daughter is forty years old and the mother is still judging her, criticizing her, and making statements of disapproval. The adult child returns each holiday, hoping this time that Mother will show her some sign of acceptance or approval. And each time she visits, the pain etches its way deeper into her heart.

Favoritism

Favoritism can produce the same outcomes as rejection. If children are favored or given special attention, they can feel completely rejected when another person they are close to—such as a sibling or a peer—is chosen as a favorite or given special attention. This creates an environment in which a child must compete for the parent's attention or affection. Envy can become a destructive poison in such a person's life.

Children who have grown accustomed to being favored can feel they are not good enough if someone else they are close to begins to receive the special attention. I once ministered to one man who was a twin. His parents only wanted one child, so his brother was allowed to live with Mom and Dad while he was sent to boarding school. He became an alcoholic and at one point had attempted suicide. He later died of liver disease.

Betrayal

When trust is broken in a relationship, a person can become very cynical, which can result in the person being guarded to the point of losing the capacity for intimacy.

Negative Self-Talk

The lies we believe about ourselves are reinforced when we repeat them to ourselves over and over. The lies are given even more power over us when we repeat them to others.

Abuse, Neglect, and Unconfessed Sin

We have an enemy. Satan will use anything at his disposal to keep us from becoming who God intends us to be. We have ministered to many Christians who would rather be taken home to the Lord instead of enduring life on earth as they know it. These people need the Word of God to inhabit their spirit: "The thief does not come except to steal, and to kill, and to destroy. *I have come that they may have life, and that they may have it more abundantly*" (John 10:10). The Lord is not speaking about life in heaven when He says He has come that "they may have life ... more abundantly." God cares about our life on earth also, because each of us has been put here for a purpose. We have ministered to hundreds of people who have come to revelation knowledge of this particular verse in Scripture and have begun to enjoy life more abundantly.

Working through these principles is not something you can accomplish on your own. If you think you can do this yourself without the help of another, please stop reading now, and repent of your pride. I have rarely seen anyone go to their place of pain on their own and do it objectively. If you have told your story dozens of times to others and remain stuck, please stop now, and repent of your self-pity. The Word of God is clear about finding help in the prayer of another righteous person: "Confess your trespasses to one another, and pray for one another, that you may be healed. The effective, fervent prayer of a righteous man avails much" (James 5:16).

CHAPTER 2

Spiritual Bondage

It is common knowledge that we are created as triune beings: body, soul, and spirit. The Bible tells us that God is spirit, and those who worship Him must worship in spirit. The Bible also tells us that God is unseen. The essence (the reality) of the entire creation is unseen. And so it is with humans. The essence of each and every one of us lies in our unseen spirit. Our bodies and our minds will perish, but our spirits—our essence—live for eternity.

Our spirit being is projected to others through our demeanor, personality, and behavior. All of us know someone who has been saved, and a few years later, those who knew the saved person before their spirit was made new in Christ remark how the born-again Christian "isn't even the same person." And they're right. The person looks the same on the outside, but the essence of that person—the real person—has changed dramatically. Many of us need to have our spirits set free from bondage in order for us to become who God dreamed we would be when He fashioned us in the womb.

The human spirit is susceptible to several forms of inhibiting agents which, if left un-addressed, can become bondage. Lies from the enemy, what we tell ourselves, what others tell us, the effect of rejection or other forms of emotional pain, the effect of guilt or shame, suppressed anger, the consequences of sin in our lives ... all these things and more have the potential to become spiritual bondage. A person could be in bondage to a spirit of shame, rejection, condemnation, or any number of other negative forces, which can manifest themselves in many different outward signs. The process of dealing with spiritual bondage through prayer is what differentiates ministry from traditional counseling.

Counseling is often a process of cognitive reasoning or behavioral therapy over an extended period of time. Our program asks the seeker to pursue complete healing, which includes relationship with God and His power. Ministry, then, is the application of biblical principles to resolve a conflict or issue by applying the redemption of the cross through prayer and asking the Lord to heal us. A spiritual bondage can be identified when God's principles have been violated.

A spiritual bondage is not necessarily demonic, although it may be. More commonly, a spiritual bondage is the result of false beliefs, wrong choices, or even ignoring biblical principles. This produces a belief system that affects the personality and behavior in negative ways. These influences then enter our human spirit and eventually become spiritual bondage. As a result, we may live an area of our lives *driven by the flesh*, rather than being *led by the Spirit*: "For as many as are led by the Spirit of God, these are sons of God. For you did not receive the spirit of bondage again to fear, but you received the Spirit of adoption by whom we cry out, 'Abba, Father'" (Romans 8:14–15).

There are many different types of spiritual bondage, and an individual may identify with more than one of them. It is necessary for us to acknowledge and accept who we are and where we came from in order to address each problem and bring healing to the whole person. This is often the process one goes through with a Counselor, and many times this is a necessary step on the road to healing before we are ready for ministry. The goal is to bring each person to a closer revelation of who they are in Christ. When these problem areas from the past are broken and the seeker is released from the power of these bondages, he or she experiences the ability to believe the truth of God's Word about their being as a child of God. The good news is, "where we came from does not have to be who we are". We have a new identity in Christ through the power of the Cross.

Helping people begin to look at various bondages in their lives is similar to leading them through the jungle with a machete—cutting away the vines, brush, and weeds that are hindering them from arriving at the cross. One by one, we are cutting away the life experiences that have entangled them. We then help them lay this bundle or heap of rubbish at the foot of the cross. Afterwards, the seeker can finally see the Father and receive what He has for them: identity, security, and peace.

The first bondage to address is unforgiveness.

Unforgiveness

This is the most common spiritual bondage. In our experience, some have a much greater capacity toward unforgiveness than others. An inability to forgive leads to resentment, bitterness, internal torment, demonization, and even chronic illness. This could be manifested as headaches, muscle spasms, or various stomach problems. Unforgiveness can also become internalized anger, eventually causing depression. If not internalized, unforgiveness can manifest itself outwardly as uncontrolled outbursts of anger.

Many times, forgiving those who have severely harmed us is the last thing we want to do. I once met a man in New Orleans whom I will call Larry. We were working in the New Orleans City Union Mission, trying to minister to the homeless. The mission gave everyone who came for meals a Bible. Many of these individuals coming to the mission knew the Bible well, even better than most Christians. Some of these men would ask us questions only God could answer. It was a sport to them; trying to trip up the suburban Christians who were coming to witness to them. Larry was one of these well-versed hecklers.

Larry's sandy colored hair was always unkempt, and his clothes were very tattered. He noticeably favored his left side when he stood, but we didn't know why. Each day before lunch, my ministry partner and I would visit with Larry in the parking lot. And each day, he asked the typical rhetorical questions like "If God is such a loving God, then why …?"

He had obviously read the Bible to some extent, so one day I asked him: "Larry, since you know the Bible so well, why haven't you accepted Christ as your Savior?"

He answered without hesitation: "Because I know if I become a Christian, I must forgive."

Wow! I thought, if only the members of the church owned that same revelation. If members of the church could only forgive, we wouldn't have nearly the marital problems, broken families, church splits, domestic violence, and addictions we suffer through so regularly.

We eventually heard "the rest of the story". Larry's older brother shot and killed their parents. He also shot Larry in the left side of his stomach before turning the gun on himself and committing suicide. Larry was the only survivor of the carnage. He experienced multiple health problems because of the gunshot wound to his stomach. His inability to forgive had festered and grown until he was consumed with bitterness.

When we left the mission, he was still in bondage to his unforgiveness. Larry's bitterness kept him from ever getting very close to anyone else, and consequently he didn't have many friends. The last time I saw him, Larry was a homeless, lonely, angry man. The Bible Larry knew so well says, "For if you forgive men their trespasses, your heavenly Father will also forgive you. But if you do not forgive men their trespasses, neither will your Father forgive your trespasses" (Matthew 6:14–15).

We had the opportunity to share the principles of what forgiveness is—and what it is not—with the residents in the mission. Larry was not a part of those studies. I pray that someday he will learn these principles:

Forgiveness Is Not ...

SAYING WHAT WAS DONE WAS OKAY

What was done is wrong. It wasn't right (in most cases). You did not deserve it. This may be the first time you have heard this. You may have even been accused by family or friends of lying about the event.

RELEASING THE PARTY OF THE LEGAL OR DIVINE CONSEQUENCES

They will be judged. If the consequences of sin have not come upon them already, they will.

SOMETHING YOU ACHIEVE ON YOUR OWN

Some of what God asks from us in the way of forgiveness seems so huge that in our own strength we can't possibly accomplish it. And we can't. Sometimes, it is only through God's grace that we can do this. So I often suggest, "Would you like to pray and ask for God's grace to begin forgiving?" It is often amazing the way His grace will flood over the person, and in minutes they are ready to begin forgiving some of the worst offenses. With others it may take days or even weeks. His grace is sufficient.

Merely Words to Satisfy Some Legal Standard

If we are forgiving out of compulsion, it won't be fruitful. Also, if we are forgiving as the result of making an excuse for someone, it will be equally unfruitful. For example: "I can forgive them because I know they had a bad childhood." This is *excusing* or *rationalizing*, not *forgiving*, and although it may seem healthy, it is ultimately not helpful.

Dependent on the Perpetrator's Response

This procedure is completely between God and us. The person doesn't have to be alive, present, or involved. In fact, rarely will the one who has hurt you be a part of this process, and then only by God's doing, and even this may not come until years after you have forgiven.

Easy

It begins with a choice and continues as a process. If there is any one thing the enemy is using most effectively to keep the church in bondage, it is unforgiveness. Most people we do ministry with begin forgiving this way: "God, help me …"; "Lord, I'd like to …";

"Father, I want to …"; or "Jesus, give me the strength to …." When this comes up during ministry time, we gently stop you from going further and suggest that forgiveness will become effective when you choose to forgive. Forgiveness begins with a choice. You may need to ask for God's grace in order to make the choice, but the choice must be made. Yoda is correct in this case when he says, "There is no try; you either do or you do not."

A Feeling

It is a choice. If we wait until we feel like forgiving, we will remain in bondage indefinitely.

Forgiveness Is …

Taking Ourselves Out of the Judgment Seat

That belongs to God alone. Most of us either don't realize—or don't acknowledge—that when we don't forgive, we are setting ourselves up as someone's judge. If we acknowledge and accept Christ's forgiveness for ourselves, we have no right to withhold forgiveness from someone else.

An Act of God's Grace Being Poured Out through Our Heart

We are often unable to forgive as completely as God would like us to if we rely solely on our own strength as humans. But He gives us the grace to go beyond what we think is possible.

A Result of Being Transformed into His Image

When we forgive, we are taking on His mind and heart, and we are clothing ourselves with Him. It is just as much an opportunity to set ourselves free as it is an opportunity to release the person who wronged us. In reality, when we choose not to forgive, we give the offender the right to continue hurting us. This is true even if the person who hurt us is no longer around. The offender has power over us until we choose to forgive.

The Removal of a Significant Portion of Satan's Ground

In the act of forgiving, we remove what has allowed our perpetrators to continue hurting us over and over again. This sets us free from their ability to damage us emotionally. It also removes their ability to damage our relationship with God and others. Do you really want to give your perpetrator continued power over you?

An Act of the Will

If we are using our free will to harbor resentment toward someone, we can also use our free will to let go of that resentment. Forgiveness need not be subject to our feelings.

A Basic Element for Deliverance

In all our times of ministry, we have never seen a seeker experience freedom without first choosing to forgive or repent or both. If someone renounces an evil spirit or attempts deliverance without considering the steps of forgiveness, they may not experience freedom. Without forgiveness, the sense of freedom is only temporary or rarely occurs.

Levels of Forgiveness

In our first year of working in the healing ministry, we noticed a common theme among the seekers we were working with: they had many misconceptions and many definitions of forgiveness. There are several misunderstandings of what forgiveness is among both people within the church and those outside the church. Most of these misunderstandings are, in truth, an excuse not to forgive, even though Jesus commands that we must forgive. Many people in the body of Christ have adopted these convenient ways of avoiding His command. In order for us to truly walk through forgiveness in the way Christ is asking us, we must walk through the pain of the offense. The following are some of the different rungs on the ladder of forgiveness:

I CAN'T FORGIVE

A woman in her fifties approached my wife and me one evening after church service for prayer. She harbored unforgiveness and bitterness toward one of her daughters. Her daughter was living with a man she was not married to and had borne the man's child. The most difficult thing for the mother to accept, though, was the fact that her daughter was involved with a black man. The woman told us she could not forgive her daughter. Besides the fact that this woman was judging her daughter, she was in bondage because of her inability to forgive. We listened and eventually asked the woman if she was willing to ask God for His grace to begin forgiving. She prayed and asked for God's grace. In less than a minute, she began to pray and extend forgiveness toward her daughter.

God's grace is an amazing thing. It flows in abundance, and it reaches whoever asks for it. We have seen the grace of God cleanse many hearts, minds, and spirits, and all we have to do is ask for it in earnest, then yield.

Sometimes people make vows: "I will never forgive …." In such cases, the person will be unable to forgive until the vow is identified and renounced. Some have made a vow never to forgive themselves. When in prayer, this can also be renounced and the power of the vow broken. Forgiving ourselves may be necessary before any healing can take place.

I Can't Forgive; It Would Be Betrayal

Mary Sue was twenty-eight years old. Her short, dishwater-blond hair capped a very thin frame. She was very outgoing and worked with our outreach program in the rehab facility. She asked to meet with my wife and me because she was having a difficult time working in the rehab ministry at the time. Her problem was that the rehab center was too much like home. As she told us her story, we learned that her father was an alcoholic. Mary Sue's situation was further complicated because her mother regularly informed her of the problems the parents were having in their relationship. Her mother shared with Mary Sue the details of extramarital affairs her father had engaged in and other behaviors that damaged their relationship as well. Mary Sue's mother pulled her into the relationship more as a friend than as the child. Mary Sue eventually began to resent her father, which affected her relationships with males as a young adult.

We began walking her through some hurts she had received from her mother, and she prayed and forgave her mother of several wrongs. We then asked her if she could begin forgiving her father. "I can't forgive my dad," she said. "I would be betraying my mother."

Mary Sue had what is called a "fused relationship" with her mother. She had been drawn in as a confidante and as a result had formed an alliance with her mother against her father. She had taken on the role of protector and possibly even felt responsible for her mother. Now, at the age of twenty-eight, it was long past time for her to stop carrying her mother's burdens. A week later we prayed with her, and she forgave her father.

This is an example of bondage often found within a fused relationship. The child assumes ownership of the offended parent's suffering and an alliance is formed between the offended parent and the child against the offending party. Later in life, the adult child finds herself unable to forgive the other parent—in Mary Sue's, case her father—without feeling as though she is betraying her mother. Mary Sue was able to forgive her father as soon as she put the responsibility for her mother into the Lord's hands, allowing Him to be her mother's protector instead of assuming that responsibility for herself.

I WILL FORGIVE WHEN THEY ASK ME

Jesus commands us to forgive unconditionally. A person's repentance is not a requirement for us to forgive them.

I'LL FORGIVE THEM, BUT I'LL HAVE NOTHING TO DO WITH THEM

In some cases, this could simply be a way to punish the other person or a way to exact vengeance. In either case, forgiveness has not truly taken place. This happens all too often in the church. Scripture commands us to find reconciliation and be reunited. This doesn't happen in many instances; instead, we hear, "The Lord is leading us to another church," as the offended party evades the command in favor of holding on to the human inclination to hold grudges. *It should be made clear, however, there are situations such as domestic violence, or other forms of abuse, when it is wise to forgive but maintain healthy boundaries or distance in the relationship.*

I'll Forgive, but I'll Never Trust Them

This is sometimes a wise or necessary boundary, but it can also be another way to get revenge. If we vow never to trust, we never will. Believe it or not, trust, like forgiveness, eventually comes down to a choice. Paul tells us in 1 Corinthians 13:7 (NIV) that love "always protects, always trusts, always hopes, always perseveres." Of course, in some cases it is a reasonable expectation that the offending person repent, change, and display consistent, appropriate behavior. However, we often say, "I'll never trust again," as a way to punish or get revenge. Obviously, any marriage will have difficulty recovering if a spouse says, "I forgive them, but I don't know if I can ever trust them again."

There are natural exceptions, such as a case of child sexual abuse. We do not recommend the risk of trusting a father who had molested his daughter to the point where he is left alone with his grandchildren.

I Forgive, but They Owe Me

We once ministered to a woman who suffered greatly at the hands of her father. When we met her, she was sixty years old. She was married with children of her own. Her story was horrible. When her brothers went to their father and asked him to teach them about sex, he told them, "You have two sisters. Learn from them." She went on to describe other injustices in her family and how she was mistreated. When asked if she had forgiven her father, she said she had forgiven him. I then asked, "Do you feel like he owes you anything?"

She immediately responded, "You bet he owes me. He owes me respect, he owes me shoes without holes in them for school, he owes me taking me on his lap and telling me he loves me; he owes me ...; he owes me ...." The list went on.

I waited a minute after she finished and said, "I'm sorry, but that is not forgiveness." After allowing that to settle for a minute, I asked her, "Would you like to pray and forgive each one of these specific issues?" She did.

All seekers must come to a place where we can pray, "I forgive, and he/she owes me nothing." When we look at the bottom line of the ledger, we must see a balance due of zero. Instead of focusing on what it costs us to forgive—which is what Satan wants us to focus on—we are better served to assess what it costs us if we refuse to forgive those who have hurt us the most. Forgiveness is the economy of the heart: it saves us the expense of anger, the cost of hatred, and the waste of our spirits.[1]

I FORGIVE THEM, BUT I WANT JUSTICE

This is an area which often needs to be addressed with survivors of incest, rape, or other violent crimes that seemingly go unpunished. Although the world declares that we have the right to see a perpetrator come to justice, our need to see justice done can hinder our ability to forgive. Jesus willingly laid down all His rights as the Son of God and died on the cross for *all* sin. When we demand justice, we are taking the place of God as judge. All who sit in judgment of others will have to give an account of this to God in the end. We are wise to let God be the judge. He alone is qualified.

I Forgive Them, But I Want Revenge

In the same way our need for justice can hinder forgiveness, our need for revenge can have the same effect. Scripture specifically tells us that vengeance is God's, and *He will repay*. His word guarantees that in the end, no one will get away with anything. We can forgive a person on multiple levels, but if we are still hoping for an opportunity for revenge, we have not completely forgiven them. Our time on earth is fleeting compared to eternity. It's simply not prudent to willingly hold on to something on earth only to pay the cost for eternity.

I Can Forgive Because …

To say, "I can forgive because …" is an act of adult reasoning or justifying wrong behavior, rather than a place of actual forgiveness. Some examples of this include: "I can forgive because he didn't mean to …," or "He was drunk at the time," or "My mother had a terrible childhood," or "She did the best she could." None of these express the true meaning of forgiveness. In fact, they actually devalue forgiveness. They are excuses we make for another's wrong behavior.

When we assume the other person made a conscious choice to do what they did against us, and we make a conscious choice to forgive them of the offense, we are truly beginning to forgive. Forgiveness is not rationalizing what happened to us as children.

Neither is it finding ways to cope with or justify another's behavior. The unfortunate reality is that the child within us is still hurting. We must acknowledge this fact. It is okay to acknowledge the pain from rejection, abuse, or neglect. There is only one way to be healed and set free from the pain: forgive so we can move on. I often suggest to a seeker that they should forgive the person as if that person did what they did intentionally (they made a choice, so it probably was intentional). This will greatly increase the value of the forgiveness.

I FORGIVE ...

"I choose to forgive." This is the first and most important step, but this step is not total forgiveness. To find total freedom, we need to follow up forgiving an offense along with all the specific related hurts within that offense.

An example is an adult child of an alcoholic. The alcoholic parent in such a home might be emotionally disengaged, causing a child to have a sense of abandonment. The adult child may also experience trauma from things such as never knowing what was going to set the parent off, not knowing who was going to be hit or yelled at or blamed for whatever had caused the outburst.

The older child often, out of necessity, assumes the role of parent to the younger children, thus having their own childhood stolen. Often, the child is afraid to have friends over to the house because of the potential embarrassment that inevitably comes. Children in alcoholic homes often never get to experience what other children do, such as hosting a birthday party. While it is certainly not always the case, poverty is very common in alcoholic homes. Shame is constant throughout their lives. Because of reasons such as these, it is necessary to be specific and acknowledge all the different ways one has been hurt.

I Forgive, and the Offender Owes Me Nothing

This is a healthy beginning and a declaration that brings freedom. When we can pray this prayer, we are beginning to go beyond forgiveness into relinquishment. We will address relinquishment specifically later.

I Forgive, and I Choose to Bless Them

An even better level of forgiveness, is to come to a place where we can bless the person we are forgiving, pray for his/her salvation, and come to see the person as God sees him/her; precious in His sight. I have witnessed seekers come to tears as they pray blessing over a family member who has hurt them in the past. The compassion of Jesus is flowing through them when this happens.

Compassion

The word *compassion* means "suffering with." You have experienced the heart of Jesus when your heart is broken with compassion for the person who hurt you. Do not be discouraged if this doesn't happen for some time. It could take years for this level of forgiveness to come.

How Do You Forgive?

Consider taking time alone with the Lord to reflect and ask Him to show you who it is you may need to forgive. Pray and ask what, specifically, you may need to forgive. Reconsider those you may think you have already forgiven. If you have not sat with a helper and made a determined effort to choose to forgive someone of specific wrongs, it is likely any forgiveness you have done is incomplete.

We pray and ask for God's grace. We begin forgiveness with a choice as an act of our will. Our goal is to come to a place of forgiveness where no one owes us anything. When forgiving, we need to be as specific as possible within each offense. It is necessary to understand that forgiveness begins with a choice but often continues as a process. There may be days when we are reminded of hurtful events, and we may need to continue forgiving or choose to forgive again.

Example: "Lord Jesus, I choose to forgive my father for rejecting me and abandoning me when I was three years old; for not supporting me, for not being there when I needed him, for not caring, for not loving me, for not being at my graduation. I forgive him, and he owes me nothing."

I have had a number of recalls in this area even when the seeker has tried to be specific. This is to be expected. We will not cover all hurts completely in a single ministry session. There will be some new things the Lord will reveal to us in time. Most of these will be revealed through future relationship conflicts. God seems to bring about complete healing through our relationships, which is another reason community is so important. And some offenses done against us will bring hurts several years after the fact. An example would be an incest survivor who realizes—after she has had children of her own—that she cannot allow her children to be alone with the adult who committed the act against herself. In other words, she now realizes she doesn't have grandparents for her children.

How Do We Know when We Have Forgiven?

When we are reminded of the person or see or speak to her or him, and we have no negative response, we are free! In years to come we may even be able to pray for this person, and our hearts will be broken with compassion. When this occurs, we have experienced the heart of Jesus. This only happens through a deeper relationship with the Lord.

Forgiving Ourselves

I know God has forgiven me, but how do I forgive myself? Self-condemnation is another form of bondage that can be used against us to keep us from fulfilling God's purpose in our lives. Too much of the bondage most Christians live in is self-inflicted. We need to understand that when we don't forgive ourselves, we are placing ourselves above God. If the almighty Creator of the universe and the most holy God can forgive us, who are we to withhold forgiveness from ourselves? Who of us can truly say that we deserve to be in the position of judge? Did God send His Son to suffer for nothing? Jesus suffered that we might be free. This is why we worship God; because of what He has done for us.

Forgiving ourselves is as simple as this: "I choose to forgive myself for ..." This one principle seemed to work well until, a few months ago, I was doing ministry with a man who could not forgive himself even though he understood he was placing himself above God. We prayed and asked the Lord to show us what the hindrance was. Immediately, God showed us the man had made a vow never to forgive himself.

This has been very liberating for others as well. There are similar occurrences in the lives of others who have done something so terrible (in their opinion) that they immediately vow: "I'll never forgive myself for this." Until they identify this vow, ask God to forgive them for making it, and break the vow in the name of Jesus, they are bound in self-condemnation.

To quote one of my co-workers in this ministry: "If we don't forgive ourselves, we are saying that what Jesus did on the cross was not good enough for us." Wow! Do any of us want to make that claim? Of course not.

WHY FORGIVE?

Jesus commands us to forgive. If that were not enough reason, He also said that if we do not forgive, we will not be forgiven. What does that say about our salvation? Another point to consider is the fact that judging others is a sin. To withhold forgiveness is to judge. Because unforgiveness is a sin, like any sin, it separates us from God. Many who come for ministry express a feeling of being in the desert. They can't hear God, they don't feel God's presence, and the Bible offers no inspiration or lacks significant meaning. Many times, the root of the problem is unforgiveness. The person might even harbor anger toward God about their circumstances.

UNFORGIVENESS HINDERS OUR RELATIONSHIP WITH THE FATHER

Susie was a twenty-eight-year-old girl from Canada. Her long brown hair flowed easily over her face and into her thin, slender frame. Her demeanor was quiet, and she was a very compliant person. Under this pleasant exterior, Susie was carrying a load of shame. She was hurt, depressed, and very angry with God.

She had been raised in a Christian home with four other siblings. She was the middle child. Her father was emotionally distant, and Susie could not remember him ever taking her on his lap, saying he loved her, or even giving her a hug.

Her mother was manic-depressive (or bipolar), which caused her to be as distant emotionally as the father had been. In addition to the lack of love and relationship, the mother's mental health put Susie in a position to help raise the younger children. Her life was very similar to the dysfunction a child experiences in an alcoholic home. Susie had been raised in a vacuum.

Even with the huge void in Susie's heart, she did not rebel, act out, or stray like many children would. During her ministry time, we led her in prayer to forgive her father. The next day we led her in prayer to forgive her mother. That process seemed to be helpful.

On the third day, after breakfast, she made a beeline straight for me, visibly angry and in tears. When she had calmed down a little, I asked her what was wrong. "I'm angry at God for the parents He gave me," she said. I suggested she could forgive God. We prayed. She forgave. God healed. Within moments she received a revelation of God as her Father, and God helped her to understand how precious she is to Him.

We spent the next four months living on the same campus with her. She worked on her belief system over the next few weeks. We saw her every day, and before long she began to glow from within. Eventually, she became a leader on our outreach team. She truly was a new person. One day, she walked in, and I saw, for the first time, how pretty she is. She had cut most of her long brown hair off, which allowed everyone to see her face. As she grew in the knowledge of who she is in Christ, the shame she felt inside began to subside. As Christ healed her within, we saw the results in her countenance. Once she had hidden her countenance from the world because of her sense of shame; now she allows the beauty of Christ within her to shine from the inside out. She is now a precious daughter of the King. Wow! After seeing what God did for Susie, I knew I would continue doing this ministry.

FORGIVENESS NEEDS TO BE SPECIFIC

We ministered once to a petite, outspoken woman in her late forties. She had made the circuit in our city, traveling from church to church. When she met with our pastor, she walked into his office and immediately began, "I am divorced four times and separated from my fifth husband. I have been to four other churches trying to get help. What can you do about it?" The pastor referred her to us.

She made an appointment with us and came in one Saturday morning with her current husband. She shared with us that she was a survivor of incest. She said she had forgiven her father. I asked her what she had forgiven him for. "I guess I forgave him for the incest," she said.

After explaining to her the many different specifics that can be contained in one large offense, I began to ask her specific questions: "Have you forgiven him for the betrayal? Have you forgiven him for the defilement? Have you forgiven him for stealing your innocence? Have you forgiven him for robbing you of your childhood? Have you forgiven him for rejecting you as a daughter and taking you as a mistress? Have you forgiven the dishonor? Have you forgiven the disrespect? Have you forgiven him for devaluing you, for enslaving you, for the deception and the manipulation?"

I asked if she would like to begin praying about these things. She said she would have to think about it. She stood up, thanked us for our time, and left. She chose not to forgive.

Each time this woman divorces, she piles more burdens into the load she carries. Only after she begins to address specific burdens and then releases them from the load, will she be able to escape the shackles that suffocate every serious relationship she enters into with yet another man.

God Gave Us One Pill
By Andria Heese

God gave us one pill to make all our aches and pains go away. This pill outdoes all other medical prescriptions for depression, stress, pain and sickness. It trumps name-brand ointments for unhealed wounds, cuts, and bruises.

Though available to everyone, it is unknown to most of the world, and it sits in its container, unused. Some who are aware of this pill choose to take it, while some ignore it and others try to find alternative ways to get better. This pill sits in its container, waiting to be taken so we can reap the benefits, but we must make the choice to reach out our hand and take it.

Often our injuries are so painful that we feel nothing could ever heal them, especially not a pill with a warning label that says we will experience intense initial pain while the healing process is taking place.

This pill can sometimes be very tough to swallow, and you may even need someone to hold your hand while you take it. You might also need a shoulder to cry on while the pill goes to the very heart of your wounds and heals them from the inside out.

Some of your smaller wounds will be taken care of instantly, but the bigger ones take a while to heal. For some wounds, you have to take the pill more than once, because some wounds can reappear over time. Once it is administered, though, the aches and pains of the old wounds are replaced with lasting relief, contentment, and peace. The weight of these wounds is lifted from your body, the scabs and scars have been turned back into unblemished skin, and the bleeding is stopped.

By taking this pill, we are fully healed, and all our brokenness is made whole again. This is one pill that can be taken with the assurance that no shame will ever come from overdosing. It's not an illegal drug we have to import across the border; it is available to all of us and free of charge. God gave us all one pill, and this pill is forgiveness.

Relinquishment

This is giving up our right to something we feel we deserve. It can also be the act of giving up someone we may have taken responsibility for protecting or enabling. Relinquishment encompasses three distinct actions:

- To loose one's hold on something or someone.
- To surrender a right.
- To put aside a plan.

Relinquishment is not a familiar term for most of us. In its simplest sense, it is "letting go." For those of us who have grown up in the church, it is the biblical concept of "dying to ourselves." Christians also give the advice to "just give your problems to God." These are both means of relinquishment. Experience has shown, however, that most of us aren't sure what "letting go," "dying to ourselves," or "giving our problems to God" really means, and the application of these processes has not really taken place in most of our lives.

The saying "Let go and let God" has become a popular catchphrase in the church. Anyone who is truly able to do this has learned relinquishment. The real sin that hinders relinquishment is *unbelief.* It is the act of taking things out of God's control and attempting to bring about desired results in our own way and according to our own time frame. Even Abraham struggled with relinquishment by taking matters into his own hands and conceiving a son with the servant Hagar. Everything we try to accomplish in the flesh by manipulation and control will only make the situation worse. Stop it! Look at all the negative consequences experienced by Abraham and the descendants of Isaac—the child of the promise—brought about by the birth of Ishmael and then his descendants.

The mother of a young man addicted to drugs took our class many years ago. She knew he was going to kill himself if something didn't change. After learning about relinquishment, she fell to her knees and repented. While she was praying, she received a vision from the Lord. In the vision, she was holding on to her son by one hand while he hung over the side of a bridge. The Lord was standing at the bottom, telling her to let go of her son. She argued, "But Lord, if I let him go, he will fall to his death."

Again Jesus said, "Anna, let him go." Eventually she let go.

As she released her son's hand, she said to the Lord, "I can't save him. Only You can."

This vision happened a few days before Christmas. Her son came to her house on Christmas Day. She asked her son's forgiveness for trying to control him and for not treating him as an adult. She said, "Robert, I prayed for you, and I released control of your life into the Lord's hands."

He stopped her and asked, "When did you do that?"

"Monday," she responded.

"What time?"

"About ten o'clock," she said.

"That is when Jesus revealed Himself to me," he said. "Mom, I am free. My addiction is gone."

Robert married the girl he was dating. The last we heard, they have a child, and he is doing well, maintaining a steady job.

RELINQUISHING A RELATIONSHIP

If we have lost relationship with someone, we may need to let them go. Loss of relationship can happen through a break between people or life circumstances such as a close friend moving to another state or even dying. Friendships fall apart, families move away, relationships break up, and loved ones pass on. Bondage comes when we hold on to the rights to these relationships in our hearts and refuse to release them.

Example 1: A child may have difficulty releasing the right to having her biological father with her at all times. The father may have even abandoned his biological children and chose to spend all his time with his new stepfamily. The biological children might carry resentment for this type of offense well into their adult lives. One option for healing, which brings incredible freedom, is releasing one's father to the other family and giving up one's right to the relationship.

Example 2: We may need to grieve over the loss of a friendship. Sometimes life circumstances cause us to say good-bye to friends for what turns out to be the rest of our lives. It can be very helpful to pray and release those relationships to the Lord. Otherwise we could feel a sense of loss well into the future and not understand why. This kind of loss could affect relationships in the present, causing us to remain distant or to fear getting too close.

I experienced such a loss and did not realize it until several years later. As my wife and I were driving down the highway near our home, an empty feeling came over me. It was a combination of both grief and feeling homesick. I soon realized that my feelings concerned Bruce and Trevor, young men we had spent several months working with in missions. We had become very close during that time. In fact, they were like family to us. When our outreach was finished and we all went our separate ways to new commitments, we said our good-byes and flew to different parts of the world. Now, several years later, I was experiencing the loss of those relationships. I needed to allow myself to grieve over that loss. When we got home, I called some co-workers in our ministry and asked if they could do some ministry with me. They assisted me in praying through this loss and releasing Bruce and Trevor to the Lord.

This grieving is probably a more natural process for women. When women experience a loss like this, they are much more likely to cry and grieve. Men are not so quick to grieve. We just get on the plane and leave.

Example 3: Close family members who have died. It can be very difficult to release these people to the hands of God. The final stage of a healthy grieving process is letting them go, which can seem almost impossible at times. We must, though, or the burden will eventually become more than we can bear. In order for us to be healthy, we must release them to God, so He can take care of them and we can be free. A twin can feel an incredible burden if the other sibling has died. The surviving twin may eventually also want to release this sibling to God.

Example 4: Experiencing a miscarriage, a child being stillborn, or an abortion. We must release these children and be free of any guilt we may feel. Many times, the mother will blame herself for miscarriages or children who are stillborn. Sometimes, women can even believe it is God's way of punishing them for something. Release the child, and be free. Jesus came to earth that we might be set free from *all* bondage. In the case of abortion, confess the sin, and accept forgiveness. The sin is not unforgivable. Jesus died for that sin also. We can experience real peace by releasing these children and be free of any guilt we may feel, allowing time for the grieving process to run its healthy course. After a healthy period of grieving, walk in the freedom Jesus accomplished for you on the cross.

REDEMPTION FROM A BROKEN RELATIONSHIP

Seekers can take time to consider who they might be hanging on to, taking responsibility for, or even expecting a response from in a relationship that is not happening. They can go to God in prayer and release the other person—or the child— into God's hands. The seeker may need to give up the right to this relationship that's over. Sometimes we put so much value in a relationship that it crosses over into idolatry. Some become so dependent on a relationship they feel they have no value without it.

RELINQUISHING CONTROL AND RESPONSIBILITY

Another area of relinquishment is to release control of—or responsibility for— another person who may not be meeting our standards of living in a way we approve of. It is common for some to accept responsibility for another person's behavior, choices, or life decisions. Many times when we do this, we are not respecting the person as an individual, and we are often unknowingly enabling them to continue in their wrong choices.

When we assume this position in a relationship, we are not trusting God in regard to this person. In fact, if we are enabling, we are interfering with God by preventing the other from experiencing the consequences of his or her behavior or decisions. We are also committing a sin of unbelief and attempting to take the place of Christ as someone else's savior. We are not their savior; they already have a Savior. It would be more effective to allow them to both accept and submit to His authority.

Sometimes, the person making poor life choices is actually trying to escape from our control. Controlling parents can be the driving force behind the very behavior they want to prevent. By exerting inappropriate control and taking inappropriate responsibility for a child, a parent is reinforcing the child's feeling of not being good enough or unable to handle the circumstances of life. The parent in such cases is actually negatively affecting the child's self-worth.

Many of us have a need to control others in our relationships. Most of the time this stems from being rejected or abandoned as a child. When these children grow up, their fear of rejection or abandonment arises whenever there is conflict in a relationship. This fear causes them to believe they are going to be abandoned, and they become obsessed with resolving the conflict or making right whatever they have done wrong. This need to make things right will invariably push the other away, because none of us likes to be controlled. People in this circumstance must deal with the issues in their past, giving up control of the many times in their early years when life was out of control.

RELINQUISHING IS DIFFERENT FROM ABANDONING

Relinquishing is giving someone up; *abandonment* is giving up on someone. When we let go of someone we love, we stop taking responsibility *for* them, but we don't stop fulfilling our responsibility *to* them. We can relinquish by not rescuing a person from consequences (legal or financial) but continue to support them spiritually and emotionally. We can cease trying to control, condemn, and enable them while maintaining a loving relationship of compassion, empathy, and communication.

When you are able to release someone into God's care, you are set free from inappropriate responsibility, the associated guilt, and the emotional roller coaster that accompanies the attempt to control something that in the end is beyond your control. The act of letting someone go brings freedom for both of you.

RELINQUISHING OUR RIGHTS

Society will continually tell us all about our rights. Television ads tell us about our rights. Credit card companies tell us about all the things we deserve. The world tells us we are entitled to this and we are destined for that. The truth is that, thankfully, no Christian will get what we truly deserve. Praise God. When we hold on to rights we believe we deserved, it keeps us either stuck in the past or stuck in unmet expectations of the future—both of which end up bringing us grief.

When determining whether we are in bondage of this type, we should examine the "if only"s in our lives. "If only"s are impossible and illogical demands of the past or the future, placed on either others or ourselves while in the present. These wishful obsessions deny reality as it is now, and they are one of the most effective tools the enemy uses to prevent us from functioning rationally.

"If Only"s of the Past

I once asked a woman if she could give up the right to have had a normal childhood. She responded indignantly with her hands on her hips. "Didn't I deserve a normal childhood?" she asked.

"That was certainly God's intention," I replied, "but you aren't going to get another childhood."

As soon as we relinquish the right to that normal childhood God intended for us to have, He can bring His healing and "reparent" us Himself. When we deal with where we came from and release those "if only"s, we begin to see that where we came from does not have to be who we are. Scripture promises us that if we have put our faith in Jesus, we are new creations; the old is gone, and we are to put on our new selves. It's really true; we only have to believe.

"If only I had a different father or mother …." "If only I had someone to love me …." "If only I could have gone to college …." "If only my parents hadn't gotten divorced …." "If only I'd had a normal childhood …."

We all have needs as children. Wounds of injustice are devastating. No one should deny these truths, but we are not powerless or without hope. Regardless of what happened in the past, God is willing and able to heal us. Continuous focus on the past can become idolatry, which enslaves us in self-pity, anger, and depression. What good does it bring if we become stuck in the notion that "life" still owes us something? Unfortunately, life can never pay us back. We can't be born into another family. We can't change even what happened one second ago. Nor can we change what was done to us. What we do have the power to change—and control— is how we respond to these things.

We are all well-served to consider our situation both in faith and with logic. God tells us in Scripture that He fashioned us in the womb and that all our days were known to Him before the world began. If this is true, it logically follows that God not only chose our parents, but was well-aware of the environment we were being born into. He has had a plan for our redemption long before our parents, or grandparents, were even conceived.

Relinquishment is very closely related to forgiveness and is an integral component of the forgiving process. We have only truly forgiven when we have given up a right as it is described in one of the forms of relinquishment. Let us, for a moment, revisit the woman spoken of earlier who was a survivor of incest. She believed her father owed her respect, shoes without holes for school, love, and many other things. Her father had been dead for years, but he was still controlling her from the grave because of the resentment she harbored toward him. Her childhood was stolen when her brothers were given permission to practice sex with her and her sister. Eventually, through much painful work, she relinquished every one of her childhood rights. We prayed through each one and also gave up the right to a normal childhood. After receiving her own healing, she began to help others and share God's love in several different ministries.

"IF ONLY"S OF THE FUTURE

"If only I were married ...." "If only I could have my own business ...." "If only I could win the lottery ...." "If only I could have children ...."

These are all identity issues: "If only I could have _____, I would be complete." The fundamental problem with looking for completion outside ourselves is that when we put our own happiness in someone else's hands, we are doomed to disappointment. Our true wholeness can only come from God. We can ask God for a healthy perspective, keeping those things first which deserve to be first. When we can relinquish the unrealized future, we can be content in the present. Success is something that can come to us, but success can never become our identity.

Finding Hope in the Midst of Relinquishment
By Beth Hey

How do we hang on to hope if we have truly done the work of relinquishment? We may have relinquished the dream of one day getting married, or even remarried. Maybe we've relinquished having parents or siblings who give us affirmation, or a family with whom we can celebrate a peaceful holiday. Perhaps we've given up the desire to have a child or see a wayward teen come to the Lord. Relinquishment might involve career goals that seem elusive. It could even involve our own health or the health of a loved one.

As we lay down our rights to the people, goals, dreams, or situations that we've clung to, hope may become elusive or seem nonexistent.

Unmet Needs

In many cases those needs and desires are legitimate. The longing for relationship is part of our human DNA. The people we are concerned about sincerely need help and wholeness. Our goals and dreams might be admirable ones, maybe even desires God put in our hearts. What we must come to terms with is the truth that surrendering our will to God is the only way to freedom—and that is also part of our God-given DNA.

Along the journey, God wants us to transfer our hope from people and situations to hope in Him. In Romans 15:13 (NIV), Paul writes, "May the *God of hope* fill you with all joy and peace as you trust in Him, so that you may overflow with *hope* by the power of the Holy Spirit."

More often than not, when the Lord taps us on the shoulder about needing to relinquish, that area is on the way to becoming an idol in our lives ... if it hasn't already become one. We've begun to draw life there, and we think we can never be happy without "X" happening. We give it mental, emotional, and sometimes physical energy.

A Time to Grieve

When we come face to face with our misplaced or false hope, however legitimate the need, we arrive at an emotional crossroads. In the process of sincerely and completely deciding to let go—to fully relinquish—we face a kind of death. Not a physical one, but a death that's just as real in our mind, will, and emotions. It's the death of life as we had hoped and wished and longed that it would be. It's the death of an idea or a dream; the death of a vision.

In reality, before we relinquished, we put our hope in something or someone other than God. That misplaced hope is dashed, and it's at this very point that a transfer to authentic hope can begin.

When we let go of a hope or dream, we will experience grief. It might simply be a low-level hum of discomfort for some, but in many cases it's something much more intense. The spectrum can range from a loss of purpose and direction to deep despair. The rainbow of promise after a storm seems to have vanished.

At this point we need to give ourselves permission to grieve—to acknowledge the loss—to be human. The Lord, in His graciousness, knows we have kicked out the crutch. We're finding out how weak and vulnerable we are without that crutch which once brought what we thought was well-being and life. We suddenly come in touch with reality—not a comfortable place to be sometimes.

Who Runs the Show?

Control is an illusion. We may have control over own choices (most of the time), but we are not in control of anything outside of ourselves—not even our own destiny (sorry). While many things are beyond us, they are not beyond God. Relinquishment is an act of faith. As C. S. Lewis said, "God has not been trying an experiment on my faith or love in order to find out their quality. He knew it already. It was I who didn't."

If we are trying to make a dream or desire come to reality by our own power, we are preventing the Creator of the universe from being involved in it with us. Relinquishment is a bit like jumping off the proverbial cliff without being able to see the bottom ... and with no parachute. True relinquishment puts us in a situation where we honestly don't know where we're going to land or how we'll feel when we get there.

A Soft Place to Land

By its very definition, there is an endgame to hope. Hope anchors our mind, will, and emotions (Hebrews 6:19). God created us in such a way that we need expectancy, and there's a certain security that comes with confident expectation.

God will answer our cry of authentic hope—the kind that isn't up one day and down the next. A hope that's not based on circumstances. Paul acknowledged its importance in 1 Corinthians 13:13 (NIV): "These three remain: faith, hope, and love." Faith and hope are closely linked.

Through relinquishment, we have the opportunity to shift our expectation from this world to God, who is able to do abundantly above whatever we ask of Him. That transfer requires a choice, a risk, and a leap of faith. Nothing pleases God more than when His child opens clenched hands and gives up what lies within—choosing to trust our heavenly Father for the outcome.

Authentic hope brings joy and peace. It involves an eternal perspective. It acknowledges there's much more beyond the here and now. How do we know we've navigated this transfer? When we experience genuine hope—with our expectancy placed not on an outcome but on the One who loves us completely and has the ability to orchestrate all things.

Suggestions That Might Be Helpful in the Process

- Allow time to grieve and recognize the area of relinquishment for what it is—a loss, a deep disappointment, an emotional death.

- Acknowledge any anger toward God; ask forgiveness for trusting more in yourself and in others than in Him.
- Ask for an eternal perspective.
- Find Scriptures that speak of hope: memorize and meditate on them; pray them and make them your own.
- Ask the God of hope to fill you with hope ... maybe on a daily basis!

Idolatry

Anything we escape to—or run to—instead of God, and anything that takes priority over God in our lives, is idolatry. Drugs, alcohol, materialism, sex, video games, relationships, food, golf, careers, etc. ….

Years ago, we reached out to a young man we had befriended in our church. Tim had recently gone through a divorce and had begun drinking heavily. Eventually, as you might guess, he stopped going to church. We tried reaching out to him on different occasions, with no success. He was always glad to see us but wanted nothing to do with church or God. At one point, he had lost his driver's license and was riding a bicycle. My wife saw him riding his bike one day and stopped to visit with him. We went to missions shortly after that and were gone for five years. After returning from missions, I was pleasantly surprised to see him back in church.

Carla and I were hosting an Oaks of Righteousness classes in our home, and I invited Tim to join us. He agreed to come and was under the influence the first six sessions he attended. He was absent on the seventh session, so I called him, and we met for coffee at a local restaurant. We were scheduled to have a ministry session with a woman in her thirties the next evening, and I encouraged him to come and observe. I asked him to come and simply watch, to see if what we were doing was something he might benefit from.

Tim came to the ministry session, and he watched as the woman shared her shame and condemnation from two divorces and an abortion. He watched, firsthand, while the young lady was set free from her shame and condemnation and began to be transformed into a new creation in Christ. After witnessing the transformation taking place before him, he would not settle on waiting for his own ministry session—he had to be next.

We prayed with him through the loss of his father when he was a teenager, his divorce, and the forgiveness of various hurts in his life. We could see some help had come for Tim but didn't see the life-changing freedom that is experienced by many. Carla then asked him to pray and ask forgiveness for the idolatry in his use of alcohol. That was it. Deliverance came. His life was changed, and Tim was redeemed. He received a revelation of the Father. He was not abandoned or forsaken any longer; he was a son of *the Most High God*.

Tim was able to resume his former job at the Christian bookstore selling Bibles. To his customers, he was known as the Bible-pusher. A few months later, he met a very sweet woman, and they married. God blessed them with a son, and Tim never had another drink. Our friend died from cancer a year after his son was born, but it would be a mistake to focus on his death. We focus on the life he lived after being set free of his idolatry. We rejoice in the way he served the Lord for the remainder of his time on earth and the way he shared Christ every chance he got.

> Therefore consider the members of your earthly body as dead to immorality, impurity, passion, evil desire, and greed, which is idolatry. (Colossians 3:5, NASB)

Condemnation

This can come from others' expectations of what we "should have done" or "should *not* have done" or simply from not living up to our own standards.

"I should not have done that …." "I should be getting better grades …." "I should not have taken drugs …." "I should not have had an abortion …." "I should do a better job of respecting my parents …."

These are all statements that contain an element of truth, but when we dwell on them, they can bring condemnation. They may be a mask of good intentions, but they will never bring change. Statements such as these cause shame, guilt, failure, depression, anger, and self-loathing. These statements keep us locked in a continual cycle of failure and regrets (as commonly seen in cases of substance abuse). The source of this condemnation could be people in authority, our peers, and sometimes even a culture that places demands and expectations on our lives. Demands and expectations in and of themselves are not inherently bad, but they can become burdens under certain circumstances (for example, the Pharisees).

If someone has been repeatedly put down, criticized, or told what they should do, what they should be, what they should have done but didn't, or what they should not have done but did, they can break under the weight of condemnation. If a person has an authority figure in their life who criticizes everything they attempt, they will obviously see themselves as a failure and can believe they are unredeemable. This authority figure who ministers condemnation can be an employer, a spouse, a parent, a teacher, a coach, or even a peer or relative.

Condemnation can sneak up on someone slowly as it attacks like a cancer and forms a grip on a person. It can become crippling. A person under condemnation can become overcome with shame and a sense of inferiority and can even experience loss of identity. Such people can believe they have no value and can easily slip into depression. They can lose hope, and some will become suicidal.

Inner Vows and Pledges

These have often been made when we were young. They can blaze a trail for our wrong choices in life. These come in the form of statements like "I will never get married," "I will never have children," "I will never let anyone get close to me again," and "No one will ever hurt me again."

A vow is a solemn promise that commits us to a behavior, a course of action, or a way of thinking. Vows become part of our belief system. We bind and hinder ourselves with vows such as "I'll never get married" or "I'll never have children" or "I'll never trust a man again."

What about good vows? When we do sin and then vow, "I will never do this again," we have good intentions, but we immediately condemn ourselves. When we vow never to do it again and then break the vow, we have failed to live up to our own standards. When we break God's standards, we can go to Him for forgiveness and redemption. Where can we go when we fail against our own standards? We are stuck. Therefore, even vows with the best of intentions can lead us into condemnation and shame. I know your next question. What about a marriage vow? Marriage vows are fine if you don't break or violate the vow. Then you will need ministry.

> If a man makes a vow to the Lord, *or swears an oath to bind himself by some agreement,* he shall not break his word; he shall do according to all that proceeds out of his mouth. (Numbers 30:2)

Brother Lawrence was a man who pursued holiness with an amazing zeal. He came to a clear understanding of both his own powerlessness against sin and the redeeming work of the cross. His biographer wrote about Brother Lawrence: "When he had failed in his duty, he only confessed his fault, saying to God, 'I shall never do otherwise if you leave me to myself; it is you who must hinder my falling and mend what is aimless.' After this he gave himself no further uneasiness about it."[2]

INNER VOWS AND PLEDGES

"For as he thinks within himself, so is he" (Proverbs 23:7, NASB).

An inner vow is an unspoken determination we have made in our heart. Inner vows are different from spoken vows in that they are nonverbal and therefore go frequently undetected. Either form of vow can exert equal power in our lives. They can arise from traumatic life experiences and often occur very early in life. An inner vow made as a child can settle deep in our heart, where it lies forgotten by our conscious mind but continues to guide the course of our life. A distinctive mark of an inner vow is a strong resistance to change; consequently, we rarely outgrow them. Inner vows have the power to blaze a trail for decisions we make in our adult lives and can direct the course of our life the same way that a railroad track directs a train.

Inner vows may be at the root of—or work together with—compulsive behavior, bitter root judgments, hidden resentments, fears, and woundedness. Make no mistake, inner vows are often the missing key to one's healing. The stubborn resistance to change, until recognized and broken, may be what blocks release in other areas.

Most of us are completely unaware of the many vows we've made in adolescence. Most of them are never spoken out loud but instead are decisions of the heart. We observe how others are living, how those close to us hurt one another, or the mistakes others have made, and in our heart we make a vow about something, which then continues to direct our choices in life even after we have forgotten the events that led us to make the vow in the first place. Many times, the behavior we don't understand in ourselves is the result of an inner vow we made in our youth.

While Carla and I were working in Chile, we came across a young man who, because of his life experience, had vowed never to get married and never to have children. As a result of this vow, he had arranged for four abortions with different girlfriends. His vow was causing devastating consequences for not only himself but others as well. A young woman we met in Chile had suffered through such difficulty in her relationships with young men that she eventually opted to give up on heterosexual relationships and began to pursue same-sex relationships exclusively. To willingly engage in habitual sin will never bring about healing, because we are shutting out the Holy Spirit, who is the only source of complete healing.

Inner vows can have tremendous power over us until we identify them and renounce them. We ministered to a husband who had made a detrimental vow when he was eighteen years old. His fiancée had broken up with him and married another man. As a result of that rejection, he vowed never to let anyone get close to him again. This was a defense mechanism, caused by a fear of rejection. His wife of thirty years was in the room when he revealed the vow he'd made all those years ago. She gasped and made a sound like she'd been hit in the stomach and said, "No wonder we've had such a difficult time becoming one in our relationship." He had committed adultery with more than thirty-five other women during their thirty years of marriage. His fear of rejection, which prompted the vow, prevented him from trusting God, which never allowed him and his wife to become one flesh as God had intended. The man's wife ran into Carla by chance a few years later. She thanked my wife for the ministry they'd received and said their marriage was made new. "I love my husband," she exclaimed, "and my husband loves me!"

As mentioned in the forgiveness section, vows can prevent us from forgiving ourselves. Saying "I'll never forgive myself," removes God from the judgment seat and counts as nothing the sacrifice Jesus made at the cross. If we have vowed to never forgive ourselves, we will never be free from regrets of the past. I would encourage you to pray and break the vow so you can receive the grace to forgive yourself.

Bitter Root Judgments

Bitter root judgments are judgments we make about others. For example, "I will never be like my mother" and "I will never marry someone like my dad" are judgments made as a consequence of our resentment toward someone who has hurt us. If a young girl, for example, lives under a critical father, she may judge all men to be critical by nature and treat them accordingly.

Example 1: We ministered to a woman who had made a vow never to marry someone like her dad. When she came to us, she was on her second marriage, and she was experiencing the same things she had watched her mother tolerate for so long with her father. She was angry at her present husband, but she was much angrier with herself. She had also vowed that she would not be like her mother and tolerate abuse in her own relationships. After working with us and being led through the redemption, her relationship with her husband improved considerably.

Example 2: Another woman had been molested by her father. She had made the vows, "No man will ever tell me what to do," "I will never submit to a man," and "I will never respect a man." You can guess how her life and marriage were going. She was able to break the vows and judgements, and begin respecting her husband. Life improved a great deal in that home.

THE SIMPLE LAWS OF GOD THAT AFFECT OUR LIVES

"We will receive judgment in the same areas of life in which we have handed out judgment against others" (Matthew 7:12,). "Therefore, whatever you want men to do to you, also do to them, for this is the law and the prophets." The laws of God will operate whether we are aware of them or not—whether we believe them or not.

Whatever we sow, we will reap. This is another law of God (see Galatians 6:7) that is as certain as Newton's law of gravity. When we sow a seed of judgment against another, it has the potential to multiply and cause much torment in our lives. The longer a judgment continues unrepented and unconfessed, the greater the power it accumulates.

CONSEQUENCES OF JUDGMENT

Judgment is made and registered in the spirit. It becomes an expectation, such as "that is the way parents are" or "that is the way men are" or "that is the way authorities are." These judgments are referred to as "bitter root" because they are created and fostered out of unforgiveness.

When we harbor a bitter root judgment against someone, the same judgment is projected into our other relationships, especially close ones such as marriage. There is often a negative expectation that our spouse (or others) will show the same characteristics as the person we have harbored judgment against. Hebrews 12:15 (NIV) states: "See to it that no one misses the grace of God and that no bitter root grows up to cause trouble and defile many."

We can also project a similar judgment onto God. We can know in our mind the truth about God's character, but our heart may have trouble believing it. Our perception of God is based on life experiences with people in authority, and instead of believing God's character to be as the Bible describes it, we can project aspects of their character onto Him.

Curses

Curses are often the result of negative words spoken over us. When an authority figure or even a peer speaks negatively over us, we may internalize the negative statement by repeating it to ourselves over and over. Doing so can result in this negative statement seeping deep into our spirit, thus becoming an integral part of our belief system. This sarcastic or negative comment can have the power of a curse. Now the curse is part of our belief system, as it attaches to our spirit, affecting our personality, our behavior, and even our health.

> But no man can tame the tongue. It is an unruly evil, *full of deadly poison*. With it we bless our God and Father, and with it

we curse men, who have been made in the image of God. Out of the same mouth proceed *blessing and cursing*. My brethren, these things ought not to be so. (James 3:8–10, NASB)

The following are examples of "curses of death" spoken over children who had no knowledge of the power that drove them to a destructive lifestyle.

"I wish you had died on the operating table."

I met a boy in a homeless mission in New Orleans whose mother had told him this. He spiraled into alcohol and drug abuse and ended up as a resident in the mission. We walked him through forgiving his mother and breaking the curse. When we left the mission a few weeks later, he was leading events at the mission and on his way to being a confident young man.

"If it weren't for you kids, I could have had a career."

A mother spoke this over her six- and seven-year-old children. When I met the daughter, she was twenty-six. She was confused and insecure and believed she was unworthy of any blessings life had to offer. We ministered to her for several weeks. She was able to rebuild her foundation and discovered the confidence to continue her education, eventually graduating from medical school.

"Your brother should have lived"

We did ministry with a woman years ago whose father stated more than once. "It should have been your brother that lived instead of you." She came to us so we could pray through the curse. She began by forgiving her father for speaking this curse of death over her. Then she renounced the curse in the name of Jesus and chose to believe what God's Word says about her.

"You'll never amount to anything." "You were an accident." "You are fat." "You would make a terrible mother." "No one would want to marry you." "You're a slut, just like your mother."

A girl we met had been gang-raped, and her father said it was her own fault. She was in bondage to compulsive behaviors such as eating and shopping. She repeatedly found herself in immoral relationships. We lost contact with her, and we pray she has discovered the love of the Father's heart.

"You should have been a boy." "You'll never learn." "You are going to end up just like your father."

The effects of some curses are not easily discovered. God has a way of arranging conflict in our relationships for the sole purpose of bringing healing to us. When the irrational feelings surface, it means something is wrong under the hood. We need to take a look.

NEGATIVE SELF-TALK

This can be a self-induced curse. Negative self-talk can stem from our perception of a certain event. Example: when parents get divorced, the children may believe it was their fault or that something is wrong with them. Sometimes, negative self-talk begins when we don't meet our own standards. Not meeting personal standards, combined with a low self-esteem, produces statements like "I'm tired of living"; "Nothing ever goes right"; "I give up"; "I'm a mess"; "I'll never amount to anything"; "I'm not good enough"; and "What's the use?"

IMPLIED CURSES

These are nonverbal actions that show disapproval. The origin of a curse may be difficult to identify because it comes from nonverbal actions. These can be very subtle and difficult to define. The implied curse is the result of what we interpret from someone else's expressions of disapproval (frowns, scowls, rolling the eyes, or other negative body language). Some people in positions of authority have an uncanny ability to control or manipulate others with their actions or expressions of disapproval. Sometimes this comes from the way they ignore us or not acknowledge our presence when they walk into a room. We are compelled to make our own interpretation of what these behaviors mean, and those interpretations can hardly be positive. We receive these signals and draw conclusions that can have significant power over us.

Studies show that 70 percent of our communication is nonverbal. Disconnect and lack of interest in a relationship can signal rejection. When a child is not being admired by an adult, that child is being injured. Children need healthy attention from the adult; if they don't receive it, they will find the attention in unhealthy ways.

SARCASM, THE DECEPTIVE KILLER

Sarcasm is often used in a joking manner as an attempt to bring humor into various scenarios such as group events or family gatherings. While such comments about a person are spoken in a joking tone, it is often hostility disguised as humor. The perpetrator is having fun at another person's expense. In truth, sarcasm always has a victim. Sarcasm is a subtle form of bullying, and most bullies are angry, insecure cowards. This is another tool the enemy uses to tear someone down emotionally.

Many of us tolerate this for years from co-workers or family members. We laugh it off with the group but later suffer the effects of humiliation, shame, and rejection. The damage done by this deceptive act of humor can be long-lasting and devastating. It is another cause of a curse.

The word *sarcasm* comes from the Greek root *sarkasein*, which literally means "to tear or strip the flesh off." English professors distinguish sarcasm from irony by defining sarcasm as "cutting in nature." In the Greek language, *sarcs* are the bits of sharp metal objects bound in a whip's lashes. The *sarcs* (which were used on Jesus) were employed in torture and used to cut into the person's flesh until the organs were exposed. Sarcasm is used as humor in our culture, but it really isn't very funny, is it?

REDEMPTION

There are several steps to breaking these kinds of curses.

- We help people acknowledge the lies they have believed.
- We help them pray and forgive the person for what was said, asking them to be specific in the exact phrase, even if it is profanity.
- They must repent of believing the lie that was spoken and ask the Lord to forgive them for believing the lie.

- We help them pray and renounce the words spoken over them as a curse.
- We help them replace the lie with the truth.

What might be some of the negative words spoken over you by an authority figure?

What are some of the lies you have believed because of the circumstances in your life or from other nonverbal expressions?

The Occult and False Religions

False religions or occult involvement is an open invitation to demonic influence in our lives. This is true with anything we put faith in or practice that is not true to the Christian faith.

INVOLVEMENT IN THE OCCULT

We once worked with a woman in her thirties who was having difficulty with confusion, insecurity, difficulty in making decisions, fear, and anxiety. We asked her if there was anything in her past that included any involvement with the occult. She was raised in a Christian home, but she and a neighborhood friend had read a book on witchcraft when she was fourteen years old. She had identified very closely with the character in the book. She thought on the book frequently and had taken some of the things in the book to heart. We prayed with her. She asked forgiveness and renounced the witchcraft. She began shaking, and immediately it was gone. She began to think more clearly in her daily life, and her fear and anxiety were alleviated.

> There shall not be found among you anyone who makes his son or his daughter pass through the fire, or one who practices witchcraft, or a soothsayer, or one who interprets omens, or a sorcerer, or one who conjures spells, or a medium, or a spiritist, or one who calls up the dead. (Deuteronomy 18:10–11)

Examples of occult activities: ouija board, tarot cards, palm reading, astrology, blood pacts, or games with demonic characters.

Occult Items Still In Possession

I received a call one day from a man who had suffered an apparent heart attack. He was struck down at work and rushed to the hospital. The medical staff put him through a battery of tests and observed him for a considerable time before releasing him. They couldn't find anything wrong with his heart. When describing the event, he said it felt like a serpent had wrapped around his heart. He said it felt like his heart was being choked or strangled. I asked if he'd been involved in any occult activity recently. It turns out that he was remodeling a woman's house who died before he could finish the work. Fearing he would not get paid by her family, he took several loads of storage from her basement. Among the items he took and stored in his basement were occult books and Ouija board.

Even gifts from someone involved in occult activity can bring anxiety, fear, depression, health problems, spiritual attack, torment, and bad dreams. We should be rid of any object that could keep us tied to such a person spiritually.

We have found ministry much easier if we have seekers renounce involvement in false religions before the ministry begins. I do admit that we occasionally lose a seeker at this time, because not all agree with the importance of this process. Some have had family members in one of these organizations, and they felt it would be rejecting the family member to renounce something their father or grandfather believed in. Some have even been current members of one of the groups we list (see just below).

In our search for truth, many of us have explored a variety of spiritual experiences. These experiences may have established beliefs and values that are not true to the Word of God. We also may have opened ourselves to occult practices or demonic activity. Other religions, cults, and spiritual teachings have elements of truth in them, but they use these partial truths to lead us into deception.

One lady was a long-time member of a Christian cult church. After being saved, she was quite disturbed by the many lies she had been taught in the church. She began consuming the Bible, going back-and-forth between the Old Testament and New Testament, following every reference between the two. She hungered for the truth.

The following is not a complete list of questionable organizations which are outside the Christian faith, but it can serve as a guide to help you identify the nature of organizations that contain questionable teachings. This list was also compiled over two decades ago, so some of the organizations may no longer exist, and unquestionably, other organizations have formed since then. As you read through the list, ask the Lord to show you any that you have been involved in (knowingly or unknowingly) or have put faith in that you need to renounce involvement with.

You don't need to renounce visiting a mosque or attending a lecture held in a Unitarian building or taking a class in yoga exercise. If you are open, the Holy Spirit will reveal to you any area that needs to be addressed. If something stands out, but you are unsure, it doesn't hurt to renounce it anyway. It is necessary, however, to renounce any previous or current involvement with satanically inspired occult practices. Renounce any activity or group which denies Jesus Christ, offers guidance through any source other than the absolute authority of the written word of God, or requires secret initiations, ceremonies, or covenants.

REDEMPTION

Confess and renounce each involvement using the prayer model on page 191 for renouncing false religions, cults, secret societies, and the occult. Repeat the prayer separately for each item on your list:

From Neil Anderson's book *Setting the Church Free*

False Religions	**Cults/Secret Societies**	**The Occult**
Baha'ism	Black Muslim	Astral-projection
Church of the Living Word	Christian Science	Automatic Writing
Eckankar	Eastern Star	Blood Pacts
Family of Love	Fetishism (objects of worship)	Clairvoyance
The Family International	Freemasonry	Cutting
Hare Krishna	Rosicrucian	Materialism
Islam	Scientology/Dianetics	Mental Suggestions
Jehovah's Witnesses	Shriners	Mind Swapping
Mormonism	Silva Mind Control	Palm Reading

New Age	Theosophical Society	Psychics/Fortune Telling
Science of Creative	The Way International	Speaking in trance
Science of the Mind	Unification Church	Spirit Guides
Scientology	Unitarianism	Tarot Cards
Swedenborgianism	Unity	Telepathy
Worldwide Church of God	Transcendental Meditation	
Yoga (Religion)		
Zen Buddhism		

Also: astrology, black/white magic, Dungeons and Dragons, incubi and succubae (sexual spirits), New Age medicine, ouija board, psychic healing, sorcery/witchcraft/Wicca, séances, table lifting

THE CAUSES OR LEGAL RIGHTS OF DEMONIC TORMENT

"Like a flitting sparrow, like a flying swallow, so a curse without cause shall not alight" (Proverbs 26:2).

Much to the disappointment of demons, they cannot torment believers without legal rights. Their power rests completely in lies. If demons could do whatever damage they wanted, whenever they chose, we would all be in big trouble. They are, however, limited by the truth of God's Word and the principles set forth by God himself. There can be no causeless curse. In other words, no consent ... no curse.

Even more important than recognizing the curse is discovering the cause. Knowing the truth can be of untold benefit to believers in their spiritual walk. Demons must have legal rights, rights recognized by Jehovah God before they can gain access to believers. Cause means legal rights that demons have to torment believers. Any and all causes can be removed through repentance, confession, renunciation/denunciation ... by receiving and applying the work of the cross ... by coming into agreement with what God says. The following is a list of some common causes for a curse.

SOME COMMON "CAUSES" OR LEGAL RIGHTS OF DEMONS

- *Ancestry:* "I the Lord thy God am a jealous God, visiting the iniquity [absence of moral or spiritual values or morally objectionable behavior] of the fathers upon the children unto the third and fourth generation of them that hate me" (Deuteronomy 5:9). Iniquities of our ancestors can be a cause for curses. Recognizing and then breaking the cycle of generational sin may be necessary for some of us.
- *Lying:* Tell a lie, you might get a demon; live a lie, you have a demon! You cover it, God will expose it; you confess it, God will cover it. Believing a lie is the power of the demon. Victory as a believer hinges upon truth; victory for a demon depends upon lies.
- *Unforgiveness:* "...his master handed him over to the jailers to be tortured, until he should pay back all he owed. This is how my heavenly Father will treat each of you unless you forgive your brother or sister from your heart" (Matthew 18:34–35, NIV). Unforgiveness can be cause for a curse.
- *Anger/bitterness/hate–related sins:* "Be ye angry, and sin not: let not the sun go down upon your wrath: neither give place to the devil.... And grieve not the Holy Spirit of God, whereby ye are sealed unto the day of redemption. Let all bitterness, and wrath, and anger, and clamour, and evil speaking, be put

away from you ..." (Ephesians 4:26–27, 30–27, 30–31, KJV). These can all be causes for a curse.
- *Sexual impurity:* Sometimes this is passed on as a generational curse. Receiving or causing sexual abuse, sexual deviance or perversion, sexual relations outside of marriage, pornography, births outside of wedlock ... all of these can be cause for a curse.
- *Occult or secret organizations and their vows and ceremonies:* Pledges, vows, oaths, or ceremonies connected to organizations such as Freemasonry, Eastern Star, Rainbow Girls, Odd Fellows, Rebecca Lodge, etc., including many fraternities and sororities, can be causes for a curse.
- *Dishonoring your body:* alcohol, drugs, nicotine, body piercings, tattoos, vanity enhancements, etc., can be causes for a curse.
- *Doubt/unbelief/pride:* Although listed last, these rank high in occasion for opening doorways for demonic spirits.

Cause for curse is simply legal permissions that demons have gained through either the decisions made by our ancestors or the experiences of our own life. Remember, there can be no curse without a cause. While our lives may be indirectly affected by demonic activity tormenting other individuals, we determine what affects us directly by confessing doorways we have opened and casting out demonic spirits. There is no cause that cannot be cancelled through Christ.

There is no such thing as a "causeless curse." God's Word says they do not exist. So if a person is being tormented by demonic spirits, he or she must remove the cause. Here is a step-by-step procedure that is always true:

Cause ... Identify what event(s) gave the demons legal permission to torment.

Curse ... Identify the results from that cause. All demons kill, steal, and destroy. What is being stolen from you? What is being damaged? What is dying?

Consequence ... This is tied to the curse. What is the fruit in your life as a result of the curse?

Choice ... God gave us the gift of free will, and He will allow us to make our own choices. Choosing to hold on to a legitimate cause for curse extends the consequences; I have seldom seen a demon leave without the command to leave.

Confess ... Until there is confession of sin along with agreement and alignment with truth, the demon does not have to leave. Confession cancels permission.

Confront/Cast Out ... Demons must be cast out. They cannot be counseled or medicated out. Jesus said, "Cast out demons."

Cure ... Once the demonic spirits have been removed, physical healing often takes place, and emotional wounds begin to mend. That is God's process ... and it always works!

On the first night of class, a woman in her forties entered our house and almost immediately stated, "I have been communicating with a little friend since I was nine years old. He is about four feet tall, green, with pointed ears. Can I get rid of him here?"

I replied, "You can if you want to."

During her ministry time, she shared why she began communicating with this imaginary friend at the age of nine. She was angry at her parents for disciplining her, although they had just cause. She decided to reject her parents and refused to interact with them unless she had to. Instead of relating to her parents, she had her friend she could talk to any time. Now in her forties, the little friend was still visiting her. Now that she was Christian, however, the little friend had become an annoyance.

We led her to ask forgiveness for her rebellion and the relationship she had with her little friend. When she renounced the involvement and commanded him to leave, she convulsed slightly and lost control of her bladder. Obviously, she had to leave early that night, but she had no more visits from her little green friend.

Soul Ties

THE BONDAGE OF SOUL TIES

God created us to have relationship with Him. We are relational beings. When our relationships with others are inappropriate, we break relationship with God and directly affect our relationships with others. Soul ties can also be acquired from emotional ties or in a relationship of inappropriate authority. There is a bondage which develops from having inappropriate relationships (such as sex outside of marriage or someone taking advantage of us sexually against our will). We call this type of bondage soul ties.

> Or do you not know that he who is joined to a harlot is one body with her? For "the two," He says, "shall become one flesh." But he who is joined to the Lord is one spirit with Him. (1 Corinthians 6:16–17)

> Therefore a man shall leave his father and mother and be joined to his wife, and they shall become one flesh. (Genesis 2:24)

The breaking of soul ties is one of the simplest ministry models we use, and yet it is the most powerful in breaking the hold Satan has on someone. We have used this model to break the power of sin and shame with people who have had sex outside of marriage, been molested as children, and even survived incest. This spiritual bondage wreaks havoc in many lives, and the healing that can be experienced cannot be overstated. Several people have reported "feeling like a virgin" after praying through their sexual sins of the past.

The process of asking forgiveness and breaking soul ties may seem unnecessary to many. Some will argue, "God forgave me of my sins when I got saved." Yes, that is true, but are you free? Scripture addresses sexual sin, holiness, purity, and the consequences of sin in this area on more than a hundred occasions. This is a very important issue in the Lord's eyes.

When we got saved, we confessed in a general fashion, and God forgave us. Yes, this covered many sins and was extremely helpful. As we walk with the Lord, though, He continually urges us to let go of the sins we choose – sometimes secretly – to hold on to. These sins must be released in order for us to be holy, as God has called us to be. The following truth is difficult for us to accept: when we sin in any area, we have first thought about it, planned how we are going to act it out, and many times we even dwell on the idea before we proceed to action. We sin specifically; we don't sin in general.

We need to be as specific as we can in ministry sessions. When we ask forgiveness for specific sins, the enemy can no longer use it against us. We can then answer Satan, the accuser, when he attempts to condemn us for our mistakes: "Yes, I did that, and the Lord has forgiven me, and my sin is covered by the blood of Christ. I have been redeemed." The revelation of God as our Father is much easier to experience after we have addressed soul ties as well. As long as we see ourselves as unclean, it is almost impossible to come into the presence of the Father with a clear conscience. God's love *is* available, but we must receive it.

Good Soul Tie Can Become Bondage

Soul ties can occur through strong emotional relationships, marriage, or close friends who share openly. These can be deep bonds that form naturally, but if that relationship ends for some reason, it can cause a form of bondage. It is good to have strong and deep relationships with others, but sometimes we can give a close friend too much authority in our life. If a healthy relationship ends for one reason or another, we may need to let go of it. We will be bound by that soul tie until we consciously let it go. We might find it necessary to release a soul tie with a friend or other close relationship simply for the sake of moving on. This could be for their sake as well as our own to be open to new relationships.

The Bondage

The bondage that comes from soul ties can keep us from healthy function in other relationships. For example, if we have a strong emotional tie with someone from our past, or if we have had a physical relationship with someone outside of marriage, these ties can hinder us from becoming one with the person we marry.

Regarding Purity

Scripture tells us that our body is the temple of the Holy Spirit. Scripture also cautions us against defiling our temple by sinning sexually. The motivation for breaking soul ties is to cleanse our temple and restore purity.

> God's will is for you to be holy, so stay away from all sexual sin. Then each of you will know how to take a wife for himself and live in holiness and honor—not in lustful passion like the pagans who do not know God and his ways .... God has called us to live holy lives, not impure lives. Therefore, anyone who refuses to live by these rules is not disobeying human teaching but is rejecting God, who gives his Holy Spirit to you. (1 Thessalonians 4:3–5, 7–8, NLT, with marginal reading)[3]

REDEMPTION

In order to prepare for the ministry of breaking soul ties, take time to pray, and ask the Holy Spirit to reveal those areas where soul ties exist in your life. Consider the following:

- Are there areas of impurity (sex, inappropriate touching, lustful thoughts, etc.)?
- Has anyone defiled me?
- Have I defiled anyone?
- Are there emotional ties that need to be broken?

MAKE A LIST

It is helpful to compose a chronological list; starting with the first incident you remember and working your way to the present. Do not group anyone together on your list. As we confess each incident on our list, we come into a greater appreciation of what Jesus has done for us. It's just plain humbling. An additional benefit of addressing each incident individually is that when praying through each one, we give ourselves opportunity to address something specific that we may have forgotten or did not want to confess to anyone.

We ministered to one man who had soul ties with more than thirty women (some men have had soul ties with more than a hundred women). This particular man acknowledged taking part when one of the women had an abortion. He had also been in a sexual relationship with a married woman, which caused her to have problems in her marriage. These specific sins could not have been addressed if he had prayed to break the ties as a group.

Discard Gifts

You may also want to consider keepsakes or gifts from someone with whom you were in a sinful relationship. When we are seeking to break soul ties with someone, it is very helpful to remove the photos and other things we are keeping by which to remember them. Pray, and the Lord will reveal these things to you. What good can come from keeping items from past relationships if we are trying to become one with someone else now? Is it fair to your future spouse to keep photos of ex-spouses or ex–significant others? Keeping items that were once significant to you from a past relationship can cause turmoil; they can even draw you back into patterns of behavior that are destructive to your new life. You can always give photos and items from past relationships to children or pass them on to other appropriate family members.

> When soul ties are broken, we experience freedom that can leave us feeling pure and clean again, free from guilt and

shame. This, combined with relinquishment, can bring us the joy of newness that comes from letting someone go and moving on with our lives.

Inappropriate Authority

The most empowering prayer in the ministry of soul ties is the prayer to break *inappropriate authority* that others might have over a person. I have seen a spirit of slavery come into a child's life and exercise inappropriate authority in her or his adult relationships numerous times. This spirit of slavery gains entrance through domestic violence, domination, oppression, incest, verbal and emotional abuse, rape, etc. When we pray to break soul ties and then renounce any inappropriate authority someone has had over someone's life, the person can then exercise power to make healthy choices about relationships. We have seen healing for many people in both abusive relationships and sexual relationships they were unable to break free of.

THE SAVIOR GIRLFRIEND OR BOYFRIEND

The Lord says very plainly that "bad company corrupts good character." There is a very effective illustration of this principle anyone can perform with a chair and one other person. Have the larger person stand on the chair. While you are standing on the floor, tell the person in the chair to pull you onto the chair with them. Just stand there; neither help them nor work against them. They will never be able to pull you onto the chair with them. Then, keep hold of both their hands and tell them not to let you pull them down to the floor. They will not be able to keep you from pulling them down to the floor. In fact, you will be able to pull them down with you very easily.

We ministered to a high school girl in this situation. She occasionally would date a boy to be a witness to him. Each time, instead of her bringing the boy to Christ, the boy brought her down spiritually. Her current boyfriend was a year older than she was. The boyfriend kept pushing the relationship physically, and as time went on, they kept sliding a little further down that slippery slope. She wanted to break up with him, but he was charming, and every time he came by her work or called, she would give in and go out with him. She was a strong Christian and did not give in, but she didn't know how long she could hold her ground with him.

When it came time for her to break soul ties, she also broke the inappropriate authority. She brought all the gifts, cards, notes and photos, threw them in the trash, and came away free. She went on to become a summer camp counselor at her church. While on the bus ride to this camp, the girl sitting next to her was in the same type of relationship herself. The girl on the bus explained how she wanted to break up with the boy who kept pressuring her physically, but she just couldn't seem to break ties with him. You can guess the rest of the story. Our young evangelist friend got out her book and led the girl to break soul ties so that she, also, could make a healthy choice for her life.

AUTHORITY IS GIVEN

Authority in adult relationships is given, not taken. We can choose to allow family members, friends, spouses, supervisors, or church leaders to have authority in our lives or not. As adults, we don't have to submit to the authority someone had over us as children. When this revelation comes to seekers during this ministry, they experience freedom.

REDEMPTION

In order to prepare for the ministry of breaking inappropriate authority, take time to pray, and ask the Holy Spirit to reveal those persons from your past or present who have had inappropriate authority over you. Consider the following:

- Authority figures siblings or peers who have been dominating, controlling oppressive, manipulating, use of guilt trips, inappropriate sexual advances or acts against your will.
- Relationships where you may have felt slimmed by someone by their actions or talk.
- An authority figure whom has been over bearing toward you and you could not say no to.

Dishonor and Shame

When we fail to live up to expected standards or social values in our family or social group, we experience guilt and shame. Shame is sometimes the consequence of dishonor. We have dishonored our parents, ourselves, or the body of Christ. We also experience shame if we have been dishonored by another person.

THE PROMISE

"Honor your father and your mother, as the Lord your God has commanded you, that your days may be long, and that it may be well with you in the land which the Lord your God is giving you" (Deuteronomy 5:16).

To honor means "to respect or esteem." This passage holds a promise for honoring our parents. Actually, this is the first commandment that carries with it a promise. However, from poor choices in life, we experience the opposite: consequences of shame through dishonor. We might dishonor our family by sins we commit, and even if the family is not aware of our sin, we experience shame nevertheless. This seems to occur like the balancing of an equation and is only corrected or justified by applying God's principles through the power of the cross.

Where You Came From

A person may carry shame for years if raised in a Christian home, or a home with high values or expectations, and has have fallen short of those high values. We can also experience shame resulting from deep wounds of rejection, and others can develop an intense feeling of shame because of their past home environment.

Atonement

The absence of an outward expression of love, such as physical touch, verbal and nonverbal affirmation, or simply an inadequate relationship with parents can cause a person to feel shame. Children in a dysfunctional home often grow up believing they are unworthy of love or inadequate in some way. Others may grow up in a home environment of perfectionism and feel they can never measure up. Even though we have received forgiveness from God, we continue trying to be perfect in order to atone for our sins. Obviously, this is a futile endeavor because none of us can atone for our sins; only what Jesus did for us through His death and resurrection can accomplish that.

The Difference between Guilt and Shame

It is necessary to understand the difference between guilt and shame in order to understand the bondage of shame. Guilt is the feeling experienced when we sin against God or break God's law; shame is the feeling experienced when we break, or don't live up to, the law or social standards of our human environment. We can feel shame if we don't live up to our own expectations or personal standards as well.

Guilt is acknowledging that "I *did* something bad." Shame is the belief that "I *am* bad."

The Cause

Many will ask God to forgive them but will not experience complete freedom because they have not been released from the shame. This can be the result of dishonoring oneself, one's family, or even the body of Christ.

Shame Brought On by Sins Committed against Us

Some people are completely crippled by shame as a result of abuse they suffered as children—physical, sexual, verbal, or emotional. It is not uncommon for children to carry the shame of another person's sin against them into their adult lives. The painful reality is that we carry shame because of abuse that has been perpetrated against us, which means we suffer the pain many times over. Fallout from the shame results in our believing ourselves unworthy: unworthy of love, unworthy of respect … the feeling that we don't matter or we are worthless. Most people who deal with this kind of shame may reject themselves and struggle with self-hatred. The belief system of shame can lead to the type of self-loathing that causes eating disorders or "cutting." Shame can also result in demonic oppression, hopelessness, despair, and ultimately a tendency toward suicide.

FALSE GUILT

When we are capable of extending forgiveness to the one who has dishonored us, we can follow by renouncing the false guilt and shame inflicted by perpetrators and assumed by victims. Once this is accomplished, we are free to receive the honor meant for us as described in Isaiah 61:7: "Instead of your shame you shall have double honor, and instead of confusion they shall rejoice in their portion. Therefore in their land they shall possess double; everlasting joy shall be theirs."

REDEMPTION FROM THE SINS WE HAVE COMMITTED

The good news is that Jesus took our shame to the cross as well as our sin. The redemption provided for us through the cross is clear. We first *ask God to forgive us for dishonoring our family* (considering the family values that have been violated). We may sense the need to *ask a representative of the body of Christ to forgive us* (providing the sin we feel shame about was committed after we accepted Christ). Now the next thing is to *forgive ourselves for falling short* (provided, of course, the standard is reasonable and not an unrealistic expectation set by ourselves or others). Finally, it can be helpful to *ask our family members to forgive us for our sin* as well.

Redemption from the Sins Committed against Us

We begin by forgiving the one who has sinned against us. We renounce the false guilt and the shame we are carrying. We may need to break soul ties or inappropriate authority or both. We may need to accept and acknowledge, "This is the family from which I came, but it does not have to be who I am today." We must find our identity in Christ and what He has done for us, so we can become a vital, living member of the body of Christ. As we put on our new selves in Christ, we assume our new identity, no longer driven by shame but secure in who we are.

Redemption from Ourselves

You can be your own worst enemy ... but you already know that, right? Some of the lies you believe are from the enemy, but some you have conjured up all on your own.

> As far as the Devil is concerned, the next best thing to keeping you chained in spiritual darkness or having you live as an emotional wreck is confusing your belief system. He lost you in the eternal sense when you became a child of God. But, if he can muddy your mind and weaken your faith with partial truths, he can neutralize your effectiveness for God and stunt your growth as a Christian. (Neil Anderson, *Victory over the Darkness*)

> I am not ashamed of the gospel of Christ, for it is the power of God to salvation for everyone who believes …. For in it

the righteousness of God is revealed from faith to faith; as it is written, "The just shall live by faith." (Romans 1:16–17)

That's why you are called to live by faith. The essence of the victorious life is already true about you. Do you have a choice? Of course! Satan will try to convince you that you are an unworthy, unacceptable, sin-sick person who will never amount to anything in God's eyes. Is that who you are? No, you are not! You are a saint whom God has declared righteous. Believing Satan's lie will lock you into a defeated, fruitless life. But believing God's truth about your identity will set you free. (Neil Anderson, *Victory over the Darkness*)

Self-Pity

A Study on Self-Pity
Cindy Nichols

What is self-pity?

Pity is an emotion that has the potential to bring about emotional intimacy with others as we witness their pain. Pity can motivate us to take action on behalf of another person. *Self-pity is the process of turning an emotion inward that is meant to be felt toward others, resulting in an inability to connect emotionally with both God and those around us.* Ironically, self-pity is driven by a desire for emotional intimacy. It can become an addictive behavior as we seek the pity of others in an attempt to connect emotionally. But since it is difficult to connect emotionally with someone whose focus is inward, that need goes unmet, which feeds and increases the self-pity; thus a vicious cycle begins. It can become a thirst that is never satisfied. The danger of self-pity is that adopting the identity of a victim can become so comfortable it becomes a crutch—a crutch we don't want to let go of. As Richard Bach put it: "If it's never our fault, we can't take responsibility for it. If we can't take responsibility for it, we'll always be its victim."

WHAT CAUSES SELF-PITY?

Self-pity can be the result of

- Emotionally withdrawn parents or feelings of rejection.
- Physical, psychological, or emotional abuse.
- Feeling of sorrow or loss over unmet expectations ("if only"'s).
- Fear of other people or circumstances.
- Feeling that a situation or circumstance is a punishment from God for a sin.
- A means of punishing oneself for shame or guilt.
- A self-curse or a curse from others: "I'm so stupid … or ugly"; "I'll never be …"; "I don't deserve …."
- A behavior that is modeled by a parent, which becomes a generational sin.
- A lack of hope.
- Self-pity may be the result of an offense done to us by another person.

Recognizing Self-Pity

Self-pity is most often revealed in our words and in our thoughts. The following are some ways to identify signs of self-pity:

- Repeatedly telling others, sometimes even strangers, about your difficulties or an offense.
- Obsessively thinking about an offense, or the person who offended you.
- Asking, "Why did this happen to me?"
- Feelings of being treated unfairly, which can be recognized in statements such as "It's not fair …" or "I didn't deserve …."
- Self-damning global statements such as "Nothing ever goes right for me …" or "I always fail …" or "I always screw things up …."
- First-person focused thoughts – "I, me, my."

Example: The parent who is distraught over a wayward child, not because the child is acting out of pain, but because the child's behavior somehow reflects negatively on the parent. This can be somewhat difficult to identify but is more obvious when we ask ourselves: *"What about this situation is bringing me discomfort? Who is the real focus of my concern?"* Listen to yourself, and be aware of your emotions as you think about the situation. Do you feel shame or guilt (self-pity), or do you feel compassion for the child's pain?

Comparison and Envy

When we compare ourselves to another person, especially in areas we are lacking, or when we are envious of another person, we are in essence saying, "Poor me, I don't have ... it's not fair." Proverbs 14:30 (NIV) says, "Envy rots the bones." Comparison and envy break off relationship and create isolation—the opposite of emotional intimacy.

Pride

Sometimes pride is a shield behind which self-pity hides. Sometimes when we have endured a horrific offense against us, we feel a sense of pride in telling others about how we have "overcome." Our own strength or resolve becomes the focus of others' praise when we recount the story; but self-pity is lurking beneath the "apparent strength" nonetheless.

Biblical Examples of Self Pity

Many Old Testament characters are full of fear and self-pity.

- Elijah: After Elijah presides over the Lord's destruction of the prophets of Baal, Jezebel threatens Elijah and he runs in fear. He sits under a broom tree and makes his plea: "I have had enough, Lord …. Take my life; I am no better than my ancestors" (1 Kings 19:4, NIV).
- Abraham: After the Lord destroys Sodom and Gomorrah but spares the life of Abraham's nephew, Lot, the Lord comes to Abraham in a vision, telling the patriarch that He, the Lord, is his shield and his very great reward. Abraham responds: "Sovereign Lord, what can you give me since I remain childless and the one who will inherit my estate is Eliezer of

Damascus? ... You have given me no children; so a servant in my household will be my heir" (Genesis 15:2–3, NIV).
- Gideon: After the angel of the Lord tells Gideon "The Lord is with you, mighty warrior," Gideon responds: "But how can I save Israel? My clan is the weakest in Manasseh, and I am the least in my family" (Judges 6:12, 15, NIV).

RESULTS OF SELF-PITY

- Remaining stuck in unforgiveness toward another person.
- Continually focusing on the offense or the offender, thereby remaining in a wounded state.
- Creating a false sense of having the "right not to forgive" because of the awful harm done by the other person.
- A diminished view of God and His character which creates a belief that God has let us down, will let us down, isn't capable of solving our problems, is punishing us for some sin, or worst of all, doesn't really love us. Regardless of the wrong belief, it creates a distrust of God, which is contrary to His command for us to trust in Him.
- A sense of hopelessness or a lack of hope. Hope is the belief that something desired is obtainable. Hope also requires trust and reliance on God.

As we look at the definition of hope, we find in it three basic elements: confidence, expectancy, and security. Because hope is confident, secure, and expectant, it creates in us an attitude of openness toward God, toward other people, and toward life. This is extremely important, because we receive what we expect, and we receive only what we are open to receiving. When we don't have hope, we are pessimistic—expecting the worst. Therefore, we put up protective barriers against the abundance of life, against people, and against God. Then we wonder why we never seem to receive anything.

POSSIBLE RESULTS OF HOPELESSNESS

- Problems in relationships: attempts at personal relationships can be futile because we are afraid to commit ourselves in trust to another person. We have no confidence, because we fear what we have to offer the other person will not be valued, will not be appreciated, or will not be responded to in a positive manner. Either we do not reach out to the other person, or we do not allow them to reach us. Hopeless people lack assurance that God values what they have to offer Him and also feel that God will not respond to them.
- A general sense that everything is beyond our control: When we feel like we have no ability to change our circumstances, we begin to blame others for our problems and do not accept responsibility for how we may have contributed to the circumstance.
- When we feel there is no hope, we develop a self-centeredness for emotional survival.
- Hopelessness leads us to ignore other people's emotions.
- Hopelessness becomes a curse we bring on ourselves and can become a stronghold of the enemy.
- Hopelessness creates bitter root judgments from comparison and envy of those God seemingly favors.
- Hopelessness prevents us from praising God.
- Hopelessness brings about depression and despair.

Redemption

Like many bondages, self-pity is one that must be confronted. To find release from hopelessness, despair, or depression, begin with making a list of "what the world owes you"—parents, government, God, whoever. Begin relinquishing your rights to all you feel you've been robbed of. Give up the right to everything you thought you deserved but did not receive (be specific).

Forgive others who have wounded you. Confess the sin of self-pity. Ask God to forgive you for misjudging His character, for blaming Him, and for doubting His sovereignty, goodness, and kindness. Confess and repent of your feeling of hopelessness, disappointment, fear, or anger. Relinquish your right to self-pity. Ask for the grace—or ability—to hope.

Generational or Hereditary Sins

Generational sins are recognized family patterns such as alcoholism, divorce, adultery, illegitimate births, and others. We receive from our parents—and then pass on to our children—family values, belief systems, blessings, curses, and patterns of behavior. The manner in which we handle conflict in the family, forms of discipline, and family rules and responsibilities are preserved. Both the good and the bad are passed on from one generation to another.

The consequences of a parent's sin will bring some kind of wound to the children. When the children become adults, they in turn hurt their children in similar ways, and the consequences get passed on to the next generation. It is only through the intervention of the cross that the cycle can be broken and the consequences can be replaced with blessings.

Some generational sins, such as alcoholism, are easy to see. However, some families with a history of alcoholism mistakenly view their present lives without alcoholism as breaking the cycle of sin. What they have overlooked, though, is the root cause of the alcoholism, which is numbing or medicating pain through compulsive behavior. The children may not have inherited the alcoholism, but they have inherited the addictive personality and find different compulsive behaviors through which to numb their own pain. The second and third generations simply substitute one compulsive behavior for another.

The good news is that, whatever we have struggled with or identified as something that needs to be broken, we can find freedom through the power of the cross.

> I, the Lord your God, am a jealous God, visiting the iniquity of the fathers upon the children to the third and fourth generations of those who hate me, but showing mercy to thousands, to those who love me and keep my commandments. (Exodus 20:5–6)

We ministered to one family that the wife was second generation illegitimate child, her daughter was third, and the granddaughter was fourth. We have had some seekers ask to break this pattern for their children. I have not seen this to be effective. Our children need to come to Christ and break the curse themselves. This is why when my wife and I were aware of what we had done to our kids we went to each one and confessed the sins of our past so they could pray and break them from their lives.

National or Ethnic Bondages

Ethnic bondages can result in negative cultural traits that are contrary to the fruit of the Spirit. Common beliefs of different nationalities or cultures are often stated and can be true for most of the people in that group. However, some of those beliefs can be absolutely untrue for some individuals within the culture. I have known many individuals who, if they were living in a different culture, would fit in very well, but in the culture they are presently a part of and have been born into, they experience rejection on a regular basis.

EXAMPLES OF CONTRAST

I witnessed an example of contrasting cultures while working on a mission base in Chile. The man in charge of construction was a missionary from Germany. At various times, his crew consisted of workers from Germany, the United States, Switzerland, and South America. A construction worker from Germany would expect to design and build a residential structure to last at least 100 years, possibly 200 years. A builder from the States might expect our houses to last about fifty years, while structures built in South America might look very temporary. The German belief in a time of decision to build would be "We are building this to last." The belief of the builder from the States would sound like "We are building it to withstand the projected loads." The builder from South America, however, would consider first the cost and then ask, "What is the cheapest material we can use to get by for now?" These are examples of different cultural views. Which is wrong? Which view is right?

Gary Heese

SEE THE GOOD

There are, of course, aspects of each culture that are beneficial and good, while some of the beliefs need the Lord's intervention and a new perspective. In our experience while living in other countries, we could see qualities in each country that reflect God's character. We could also see need for improvement in some areas, while other areas were simply the culture.

EXAMPLE OF GUILT

We ministered to a woman once who was having difficulty with guilt while living in the United States. As we helped her identify the source of her guilt, she remembered the national anthem from her native country. The anthem she sang in school every day had the citizens declare, "I will always be true; I will never leave; I commit my loyalty to my country." She was experiencing guilt because she was now a citizen of the United States, and she felt she was breaking an oath to her country. After she broke the power of the vows in the anthem, she was free to enjoy her life in the United States.

EXAMPLE OF SHAME

While working in Japan, we learned how their children, from the age of three, are driven to excel in school. College entrance exams are very difficult and competitive in Japan. Young adults who are not chosen for university bring shame on their families. Some of these students are shunned by their families or most certainly are made aware of how disappointing they are. As a result, many commit suicide if they don't make the grade academically. Japan has the highest teen suicide rate in the world for this very reason.

Obviously, Jesus teaches us to accept others and to treat them as we would like to be treated ourselves. Before we judge too harshly, though, consider a contrast between Japan and the United States. Mathematicians conducted an experiment with seventh graders from Japan and the United States in 2007. The Japanese students were put in a room together, while the students from the United States were put in a separate room. The adults wrote a mathematical problem on the board that could not be solved. The students, however, were told to solve the problem and did not realize the problem had no solution. The seventh graders from the United States gave up trying to solve the problem after seven minutes on average. The Japanese students worked for an hour before the adults finally came in and told them to stop.

When the students from Japan came out of the room, their parents said to them, "Congratulations, you worked very hard." The parents of the students from the United States told their children, "You're so smart."

EXAMPLE OF ATTACHMENT

In some European countries, such as Germany, Norway, Holland, and England, parents can seem closed off emotionally. These children may not experience outward expressions of affection, they may never hear parents express love to them, and they might never receive a hug or other sign of physical affection. Children raised in this type of environment might experience attachment problems as adults.

Common Knowledge

Personality traits from other cultures can be passed down through the generations and even the centuries after the family has lived in the United States. Some of those commonly known traits might be, "Germans are always right; the English are sophisticated; Americans are proud; the Dutch are hard-headed; Islanders are crisis-oriented." Some of these traits you may see exhibited in every culture. Some of these traits can be passed on as bondage exclusive to certain families. Passing on certain traits from generation to generation can have the same effect as curses do—and operate the same way. As children, we hear older family members make declarations about a family trait, and we receive the declarations as truth and begin to act them out in our lives as adults.

"The Malone's are tough, we can handle anything. The O'Malley's don't get mad, we get even. You are hard-headed, just like your grandpa."

You don't have to receives these negative traits or pass them on. You can break them in the same way a curse is broken.

Ministry Preparation

Dear Friend in Christ,

Consider prayerfully what the Lord is revealing to you and the areas where you might want ministry. List these items on the "Ministry Work Sheet" on the following page.

It is possible that an article doesn't seem to apply to you. That is OK. Move on to the next article. Some of the articles may contain a large part of your life and take some time to process. Feel free to deal with some of the articles one at a time. For example, if you discover there are many events in the area of "Forgiveness" to address, you may have a separate ministry time for that alone and continue with the rest at another time.

May the Lord fill you with His Grace as you begin this process.

Ministry Worksheet

Pray and ask God to show you:

1. Who in your past hurt you (consider authority figures)? Whom do you need to forgive and for what? List traumatic experiences for which you would like prayer.

2. What "if only"s are you holding on to and need to relinquish?

3. Describe any negative or hurtful words that may have been spoken over you—or any that you have said to yourself—whose power in your life you wish to break?

4. List any vows or judgments you want to confess and break.

5. List any generational or hereditary sins you would like to break.

6. List those with whom you might have soul ties or who have inappropriate authority in your life which you would like to break.

7. In what ways have you dishonored yourself, your parents, others, or the body of Christ?

8. List the regrets in your life. What you should have done (should haves) or things you shouldn't have done (should nots).

9. List false religions or occult involvement you want to renounce.

CHAPTER 3

The Road to Redemption

From the book Walls of My Heart, *by Dr. Bruce Thompson*

Redemption means *to be brought back from* as if someone else owned you. A redeemer reclaims what once was his but was lost. We have been redeemed from the hands of the enemy by Jesus dying on the cross and shedding His blood that we might live, and have life more abundantly. Experiencing new life in Christ comes from faith in Him. Experiencing *life more abundantly* comes through praying and applying God's principles to the bondages in our lives. Sadly, too few Christians are truly applying the redemption of the cross to every area of their lives and are, therefore, missing out on an abundant life. In this chapter we recognize the various elements to the process of redemption.

Revelation

This is the first step to redemption. Just as we received revelation of the need for a Savior, we can also have our eyes opened to the various areas of our lives that still need the redemptive power of the cross. However, revelation without application can leave us stagnant. Simply understanding without acting does not bring change.

Repentance

This is the beginning of change in our lives. We identify the sin and who we have sinned against; repent of our sin (which means to go the other direction); ask for forgiveness; then are forgiven and cleansed of our sin (and the guilt that accompanies transgression). This is a primary redemptive step we can use in an area where we are stuck.

Release

This is the second most powerful step toward redemption that we can take. When we release forgiveness we have withheld to those who have sinned against us, we are free from being bound to them.

Recognition

Recognition of the works of the enemy and the spirits that are possibly controlling or influencing us helps us realize the lies we believe and the control of the enemy that we can renounce.

Renouncing

Renouncing is a verbal rejection. Through this we can break our connections to false beliefs, curses, spirits that are influencing or tormenting us, vows, false religions, soul ties, generational sins, condemnation, and any other forces of darkness.

Relinquishment

This is letting go of responsibility for—and control of—someone else, or surrendering our own perceived rights, plans, expectations, hopes, dreams, and whatever else we think we deserve.

Restitution

This is paying back what we owe to someone else.

Reconciliation

This is restoring relationship with someone we have become distanced from.

Redemption

The process of redemption for any single event in our lives may include one or more of the above steps. As we go through the process, it is important that we do so with the help of another person. It is also important that we speak and pray out loud instead of simply in our thoughts. We must also recognize that the true healing of redemption comes through Christ's power and not our own strength or the strength of someone who is helping us.

We have many natural human responses that we use in order to avoid pain. When left to our own devices, we tend to dance around the point of pain and usually fail to adequately address it. To have a helper who is objectively walking us through the process of redemption can make all the difference. This person can assist us in working through difficult points and help us recognize things we might be missing. In addition, the Holy Spirit's presence where two or more people are gathered in His name is a significant part of the process that is often overlooked.

"It is with your mouth that you confess and are saved" (Romans 10:10, NIV 1984). There is an importance to speaking things out loud which has an effect on our lives that goes deeper than when we only think about things. Speaking out loud is part of the redemptive process that moves us from having thoughts in our mind to making decisions in our heart. For this reason, much of the process involves speaking out loud to forgive others, break curses, etc. (God *spoke* the world into existence; He did not *think* it into becoming a reality).

It is also important to speak out loud when dealing with issues relating to demonic forces. Satan will only be defeated if we confront him verbally. He cannot read our mind and does not have to obey our thoughts. Only God has complete knowledge of our mind. As we address areas of the occult, it is important that we submit to God inwardly and resist the devil by praying, renouncing, and breaking bondage audibly.

Christ purchased our victory when He shed His blood for us on the cross. Realizing our freedom will be the result of what we choose to believe, confess, forgive, renounce, and forsake. No one else can do that for us. The battle for our mind can only be won as we personally choose truth.

CHAPTER 4

The Helper Skills

Listening

In our Counseling School training we learned the skill of listening, but Carla and I didn't realize its importance until we started training others in ministry. One of our resources is Gary Sweeten's book *Listening for Heaven's Sake*, which was part of the curriculum in the counseling school at YWAM. This book communicates the heart of God for His people and how to be an effective helper in ministry.

An effective exercise we do in training is a listening task with three people. One person is the *seeker*, who is coming for help; the second participant is the *helper*, whose job is to listen and allow the seeker to share in a safe place; the third person in the exercise is the *observer*, who gives feedback to the helper. A particular exercise in one of the training classes provided valuable revelation. As the seeker began sharing a concern she had, the helper began to give her advice. As the seeker resumed her story, the observer interrupted and began sharing her own story and history of a similar nature. This is what the seeker shared with me afterward: When the helper began giving advice, the seeker began to shut down. When the observer shared her story, the seeker completely closed off. The most disturbing revelation to the seeker was that she recognized she had been doing the very same thing for twenty years with those who had been coming to her for help.

Any Healing Is Holy Ground

The listening skills used in applying these principles are an essential element of the personal healing ministry. The development and use of listening skills may determine whether seekers will return for further help or whether we even get close enough for them to open the hidden area of their heart in the first place. When Moses was about to come into the presence of God, the Lord said to him, "Do not draw near this place. Take your sandals off your feet, for the place where you stand is holy ground" (Exodus 3:5). We purpose to approach the inner sanctuary of the seeker's heart with the same reverence.

Please Just Listen

I paraphrase what Jessie Swick wrote in a document years ago, "Please Just Listen."

When we are attempting to hear someone's story or concern they are sharing and we start giving advice, we are not listening.

When we try to tell them they shouldn't feel that way, we are not respecting their feelings or acknowledging the right they have to their feelings.

Worse yet, when we jump into the problem solving mode, we are not helping either and are even being disrespectful.

When a friend is seeking someone to listen, in short, shut up and listen.

You will accomplish more by allowing them to talk, and often they will come to their own conclusion.

So please listen and just hear me. And if you want to talk, wait a minute for your turn, and I'll listen to you.

(If by chance they don't, then it is still not time to give advice; just ask whether you can pray with them.)

Respect

The Lord's command emphatically indicates the need for the utmost respect. If we truly want to be effective helpers in the healing ministry, we must consider the heart of each person we minister to as *holy ground* to them. They have stuffed, kept silent, and often denied or avoided (when possible) even thinking about the hidden areas. They've attempted to escape, deny, or bury their pain in a variety of ways. These hidden areas are sacred to them, and most will remain in secrecy for decades before sharing even a general description of their past.

This was confirmed for me when a domestic violence counselor made a very profound statement I'd never heard before. "All healing is sacred," he said. Wow, that statement gave me chills. When a person is in the emotional state required for them to seek help from any kind of counselor, they are extremely vulnerable. This person in need will look up to their counselor as someone with knowledge, hoping the counselor has the answers they need. The Seeker will see the Helper as a source of hope. The Helper's duty, then, is to listen and connect the Seeker with God, the source of all hope.

ADDITIONAL BENEFITS

One of our leaders who was having trouble in his marriage bought a copy of the book *Listening for Heaven's Sake*, hoping it would help in his relationship. Not only did it help his marriage, but he received additional benefits as well. He began applying these same listening skills in his work. In a short time he was the top salesperson in the company. He received a bonus each month, and his success was so apparent that the owners asked him to train his co-workers in these same listening skills.

Another leader began practicing these skills with his son who was middle school age at the time. We all know the challenges involved with children this age. Most of them seem to have the same answer for every question: "I don't know." Our friend simply began responding to his son's comments about things that happened that day with questions like "So how did you feel when that happened?" Like floodgates opening, his son took off with a response that lasted about thirty minutes. Our friend said that his son talked to him more that day than any day he could remember. We have received dozens of testimonies from leaders who have taken the listening skills from this ministry and applied them successfully in all areas of their lives.

Listening Techniques

REFLECTIVE LISTENING

This is also known as parallel talk and parroting. Reflective listening can be used to

- Check for understanding.

- Create empathy (which is different than sympathy).
- Build positive rapport.

When we listen effectively, we express our

- Desire to understand how the person is thinking and feeling.
- Belief that the person is worthwhile.
- Respect and a willingness to accept the other person's feelings.
- Desire to explore a problem and help them understand the dimensions of the problem, the possible choices, and their consequences.

A reflective response allows us to communicate to the other person what we perceive they are doing, feeling, and saying and offer suggestions about why they are choosing their particular behaviors.

Active Listening

This method uses questions or statements to engage—not reflect—what the speaker says. Active listening is used to

- Gather more information in non-evaluative ways.
- Correct listener misunderstandings.
- Reinforce positive statements or actions.

Active listening involves engagement in what the other person is saying. It means allowing others to talk without interruptions; accepting what they say as genuine, at least to them; and not interjecting your own views, opinions, or solutions. Listening to another person for the benefit of that person is not a discussion. Of course, we also listen during discussions, but in this setting we are acting as a helping agent so the other person can unload their troubles and explore options.

Sample phrases when we think our perceptions are accurate:

I understand the problem as ...	I see the solution as ...
I'm sensing ...	Could it be that ...
I wonder if ...	Correct me if I'm wrong ...
I get the impression that ...	Let me see if I understand. You ...
As I hear it, you ...	You feel ...
From your point of view ...	It seems to you ...
In your experience ...	From where you stand ...

TENTATIVE STATEMENTS

We use tentative statements when we believe we've arrived at a place to make a statement or a suggestion. Tentative phrases can also be used if we have difficulty understanding. Tentative statements help seekers feel they are in control of the information being shared. They believe they have a choice, and they feel they are both respected and safe.

Examples of tentative statements:

I'm not sure if I'm with you, but ...	Correct me if I'm wrong, but ...
I think I hear you saying ...	You appear to be feeling ...
It appears that you ...	Perhaps you're feeling ...
I'm sensing that maybe you feel ...	Is there any chance that you ...
This might be a longshot, but ...	Maybe I'm out to lunch, but ...

I'm not sure I'm with you; do you mean ...
... Is that what you mean?
Let me see if I understand ...
I get the impression that ...

Do you feel a little ...
... Is that what you're feeling?
Let me see if I'm with you ...
I'm guessing that you're ...

AVOID IMPERATIVE STATEMENTS

Strive to avoid giving advice. Directives or imperative statements can sound like commands, or even condescension, and will cause them to put up a wall or shut down and withdraw. Here are examples of the kind of statements we try to avoid:

> You should stop this kind of thinking.
> You ought to ...
> If you would just believe what the Bible says ...
> You need to do this ...

AVOID REASONING

It doesn't help to tell someone what they need to believe, or what behavior they should stop. If they could stop the unwanted behavior, they would. If they could believe the truth, they would. We try to help them identify the cause and then deal with the behavior.

EMPATHETIC RESPONSES

> That must have been a very difficult time.
> I can tell that was very hurtful.
> It sounds like you have been through a lot.

That must have caused you a lot of ...
What happened to you was not right.
To see what you saw as a child must have been an awful experience.
I can see how that must have been devastating.
That had to be very ... painful ... hurtful ... difficult ... exhausting ... humiliating ...

DETRIMENTAL RESPONSES

Responses that question, criticize, blame, judge, disagree, warn, order, give advice, humor, shame, moralize, or sympathize can all be detrimental to communication.

CRITICAL LISTENING

Critical listening is hearing what is not being said. I probably rely on this skill more than any of the others. Critical listening is the art of hearing the seeker's whole story as if they are painting you a picture. I like to think of it as a dot-to-dot image. The helper combines phrases or comments with body language and attitude and listens for impressions from the Holy Spirit. This gives the helper a sense of the entire picture and allows us to relate spirit-to-spirit with the seeker. The helper, at some point, may assess a core belief or value for the seeker which can lead to a meaningful time of deliverance or release.

DIVERSIONS

Some seekers will begin a session with a fleeting comment about an event or behavior and then quickly move on to another person or subject. This could be a signal that something significant happened they are having difficulty talking about or would rather not deal with. (This is a rare occasion when I might make a quick note so I can take them back to that moment.)

A seeker may change subjects frequently and divert from one topic to another during ministry time. This diversion is often an unconscious protective maneuver to avoid getting too close to the pain of specific events.

Avoidance

When seekers try to avoid specifics, try to discount what happened, or try to justify what happened, they are avoiding the real issue. This can be found in statements like "I probably deserved that beating" or "I understand now because they were wounded too." This rationalizing, or justifying, is a means to avoid the truth about the abuse they suffered and avoid feeling the pain or revisiting the event that has wounded them. Wait for an opportunity to revisit that comment, and ask them to be more specific about it. Expect tears, emotion, or even anger when they are getting close to the pain of an event or memory.

The Process

There will be moments within ministry time when the seeker is mentally either evaluating or replaying an event. During the process of forgiveness, for example, some will need time to process. This is when they are counting the real cost of forgiveness. Be patient, and allow ample time for them to decide to forgive. They are making a huge choice as they revisit what happened to them as a child and calculating the injustice. They may be adding up the offenses and considering the debt that is owed them. Their eyes will frequently be closed during this time, and their head may be bowed. It is best to wait and allow them time to process. Eventually, seekers will either open their eyes or raise their head, as if to express, "Okay, I'm ready to continue." Many times I may discern during this time of processing what specific need could be addressed. If not, I simply ask, "What did the Lord show you during this time?"

POINTS OF EMPHASIS

> Notice body language.
> Notice what is being left unsaid.
> Allow them a time of silence so they can process.
> Listen for incomplete stories.
> Notice the diversions.
> Connect the dots.

Four Elements of High Performance Listening

LISTEN STRATEGICALLY

> Pay attention (active listening: repeat their words in your mind).
> Carefully select what is important (listen for points of agreement).
> Listen for the emotional message (what would they like to say?).
> Avoid jumping to conclusions.

Interpret Accurately

Have an intense desire to understand.
When in doubt, ask for clarification.

Evaluate Carefully

Concentrate on the message, not your own feelings.
Ask questions to analyze specifics.

Respond Wisely

Let them know you listened, understood, evaluated, and appreciated the information.
Clarity of response de-stresses seekers; ambiguity distresses them.

Quick Tips

- Record the data – take notes (if you feel the need to take notes in ministry sessions, it is best to do so after the session). I personally never take notes.
- Focus your efforts – concentrate. Minimize distractions. No multitasking.
- Body language – open posture. Eye contact. Affirmative and appropriate facial expressions.
- Interrupt when needed – respectfully ask for clarification.
- Mirror the speaker – rate, volume (unless they are angry), and vocabulary.
- Leverage time and location – privacy and timely procedure.
- Use time-outs when focus, energy, or commitment falls off.

- Remember *empathy* – allow inaccurate statements to "ride" a while.

Identify the Bondages

Listen to seekers long enough and intently enough to identify the bondages they are struggling with. Then help them apply the redemption of the cross to each bondage.

Physical Touch

One advantage a lay minister has over the professional counselor in a ministry setting is the opportunity to show care, empathy, and concern through appropriate physical touch. It is part of the church culture to greet people we know with a hug. It is also a custom—even a directive from the apostles—to lay hands on people when praying for them. It is the norm in American culture to greet someone we don't know with a handshake. Some have lived in homes where physical touch was absent, and this is an area in which they have been starved and neglected. The most a psychologist may do is a handshake. I had one psychologist friend who told me she learned to hug with her words. Years later I had one of our leaders in ministry who could do the same. It is a special gift for sure.

In the ministry setting, I frequently see the need to comfort with touch, even at the beginning of a session. Oftentimes, in the first session, seekers are especially anxious, nervous, or upset. I will sometimes take them by the hand and ask if we can start with prayer. This gives them assurance along with a sense of safety and care. (I want to clarify that to stroke, rub, or caress the seeker can be perceived as inappropriate and at the least as a distraction.) When praying with seekers, we might hold their hand, put our hand on their shoulder (with permission), or hug them from the side (with permission) while praying. Stroking, rubbing, or caressing can be misinterpreted as sensual and put a seeker on guard.

Physical touch might have been wounding as part of a seekers past. Kind appropriate physical touch can be a part of a seekers healing in times of ministry.

Holding In Their Pain

There are times in the midst of ministry when seekers are getting in touch with a very painful time from their past. Sometimes I hold them and simply let them cry for a while. This can be helpful during a time of significant breakthrough. You may have spent thirty or forty-five minutes just listening to their story, and during that time most of what they shared was in a matter-of-fact fashion. When you ask the right question and address the core issue, they often break and need someone to comfort them. When they have calmed down, you will know when it is appropriate to let go or withdraw and continue with ministry.

Getting in Touch

We ministered to a young woman a few times before she was able to address the hurts from her father. Critical listening was the key to healing here. Lisa Ann shared with us how her alcoholic father had embarrassed her throughout her life. The final straw came on her fourteenth birthday. Her family lived in a small town, and her parents took her to dinner at the country club, where everyone knew everyone else. After dinner, Lisa Ann's father went over to the bar and asked another woman to dance with him. She had borne the shame and embarrassment of living in a small town with most of the residents aware of her father's drinking and multiple affairs, but to do what he did in front of both her and her mother, on her birthday, was all she could take.

During her first few ministry sessions, the only emotion Lisa Ann could describe or express was anger. The problem with anger is that many things can cause that emotion. When helping someone receive the healing they need, our listening skills are the key to being effective. As we prayed, I asked the Lord to take her shame (because Jesus took our shame to the cross, we can give Him our shame). The second I said the word *shame*, Lisa Ann broke down, and her shield of anger disappeared. I hugged and held her while she cried out all the anger and shame she had been carrying for over a decade. The shield that had protected her from addressing the crux of the issue was gone. A softness came over her as the Lord met her and gave her freedom from the prison she had been locked inside for so long.

Relationship

The next important advantage of the Lay minister is the fact that there may be a level of relationship with the seeker that a professional counselor may not have. In some ways this can make the lay minister more approachable.

Father Heart Ministry

We have had some who begin a session so emotionally charged that they find it difficult to talk. They might have a difficult time even putting together a complete sentence. When this happens, I find it helpful, even necessary, to ask them if I can hold them while I pray for them. I then proceed with a version of what I call *Father heart ministry*. I embrace them, pray, and ask the Lord to come and bring His peace and comfort to them. They quickly feel a peace come over them and begin to relax, sensing they are in a safe place. In this type of setting, the seeker will begin to feel God's love through the love of the helper.

In Closing

When seekers are ready, which typically comes after they have completed the ministry to break soul ties, the Father heart ministry will be another time when physical touch can bring about much healing. As we pray for seekers to receive a revelation of the Father's love for them, the touch of holy hands can be very powerful.

If touch is something you have difficulty with, I can assure you the impact of your ministry will be limited. We live in a world where parents have mostly stopped hugging their children at about the age of nine. Some stop hugging long before then. The desire for physical touch has been hardwired within us, and we receive affirmation of our value through this expression of touch. Research has proven the need we have for physical touch in order to live healthy lives, and in many ways just to survive.

Prayer

How we pray can make a difference. My wife and I were asked to teach a class on prayer at our local church several years ago. An older couple who had been praying many years for others were required to take the class as well. The gentleman commented, "What can be so different about the way we pray?" He went on to assure us: "I've been praying for people for years." When we finished the class, our friend realized that the difference between praying for someone as opposed to coaching someone in praying for themselves can be considerable.

A TIME OF NEED

Most people have not been in a ministry of this type. Most Christians, in a time of need, are accustomed to asking for prayer and having someone pray over them. This is the norm when asking for prayer after a service or special event. At these times, people often come forward for physical healing or the healing of a relationship. And we can certainly show care and concern for them in their time of need and pray for their request.

THE CLASSIC REQUEST

The most frequent request I hear during after-service prayer is from mothers who have an adult child making destructive choices. Drugs, alcohol, sex, bad company, they won't work … the list goes on. When a mother does ask to pray for her child, instead of praying, I ask if she has released her child to the Lord. The problem could be control. Mom might need some boundaries. Parents are often enabling the child to continue the negative behavior in one way or another. Oftentimes, mothers bail out the children when they get into trouble. Several times I have suggested to the mother that the best help I can give is to help her release the child into the hands of the Lord, not blocking the consequences of their behavior. Some mothers will struggle with this for years. I pray with them to relinquish their child to the Lord and allow God to be in control. I explain that to do less is unbelief; they are not trusting in God's sovereignty.

COACHING PRAYER

I refrain from praying *for* a person. Instead, I prefer to coach seekers as to how *they* can pray for the situation they are addressing with the Lord. When someone asks for prayer, I listen to the request to discern whether it is really about a choice they need to make on their own. I can't pray for *their* choices and be effective. We learned early on that when *we* attempt to pray for *their* choices, little or no change will take place. But when they have thought over a situation and decided to make a choice, when they pray, it is as though they are making a contract with God. And in fact, they are making a contract.

If no change takes place after prayer, it is because seekers did not make a choice themselves. They simply allowed the helper to speak for them, without having the conviction themselves. Our goal is to train seekers in how to go to God on their own in order to experience real and lasting change in their lives. They will soon learn effective ways they can apply redemption themselves in their areas of need. In a nutshell, we try to coach the ones seeking help in *how* to *pray for their choices*.

EYES OPEN

I also prefer to pray with my eyes open during ministry. I might miss what God is doing if I pray with my eyes closed. It is important to watch the physical actions of seekers. Signs such as change of emotion, change in attitude, body language, eyes fluttering, or even manifestations can be a signal for the helper. Praying with our eyes open can be an awkward adjustment at first, but we can see more of what the Holy Spirit is doing when we do this.

ABUSIVE PRAYER

If you have never heard of such a thing as an abusive prayer, that's okay. Abusive prayer occurs when instead of praying a blessing and goodwill, we judge and give advice or direction about what a seeker should be doing or should have done. This is an abusive prayer! The last thing a person in pain needs in the beginning is to hear about what they've done wrong. Love must come first, before any healing can begin.

WHAT IS THE CONTRACT?

Similar to the listening techniques, we as helpers want to minister to what the seeker is asking for. Listen to assess what the need is, identify the bondage and ask if they would like to address this need in a healthy way.

Compassion

We are ministers of Jesus, and as such, we hope to minister with the compassion of Jesus:

> He [Jesus] was moved with *compassion* for them, and healed their sick. (Matthew 14:14)

> Then Jesus, moved with *compassion*, stretched out His hand and touched him, and said to him, "I am willing; be cleansed." (Mark 1:41)
>
> So Jesus had *compassion* and touched their eyes. (Matthew 20:34)
>
> I have *compassion* on the multitude, because they have now continued with me three days and have nothing to eat. (Matthew 15:32)
>
> Finally, all of you be of one mind, having *compassion* for one another; love as brothers, be tenderhearted, be courteous; not returning evil for evil or reviling for reviling, but on the contrary blessing, knowing that you were called to this, that you may inherit a blessing. (1 Peter 3:8–9)

The common denominator within each miracle quoted above is *compassion*. These Scriptures had a great impact on me, because until I received revelation through these passages, I don't believe I was a very empathetic person. Wow! I then realized that if I was going to make a difference (rather, if Jesus was going to make a difference through me), I would also need to minister with a heart of compassion. Some of you already have a heart of compassion, which is also known as a *mercy gifting*. Although not everyone has this gift, all of us can simply ask God for His heart of compassion.

For example, after about eight years of ministry, I went through a period of about two years in which I disassociated from each individual's pain during ministry. I came to realize that I was doing ministry more from my head than from my heart. I needed to connect with the seeker on a spirit-to-spirit level, so I went back to frequently asking God to fill me with the compassion of Jesus. In receiving this gift of mercy, I am able to enter into each seeker's culture, and through the work of the Spirit, I am moved with compassion for them and can help them bear their burdens. I have wept with them, grieved with them, and held them in their time of pain on several occasions. In these moments, I also feel their pain with them. While operating under the gift of compassion, we can comfort them in their time of grief as they are going through the pain of releasing and relinquishing.

> We then who are strong ought to bear with the scruples of the weak, and not to please ourselves. (Romans 15:1,)

Cultural Sensitivity

Be relevant. Often, when we are leading seekers through ministry, they themselves are not able to identify many of the specifics of an offense. Through knowledge of each seeker's culture, we can lead them through the forgiving and relinquishing of events in their past more specifically and therefore more effectively. During this process, we listen to a person long enough to identify his or her challenges and struggles. If we have some understanding of the cultures various seekers are coming from, we can then make reasonable assessments as to how we may lead them through an effective time of ministry.

Gary Heese

Confrontation

A gentle confrontation can lead a seeker to deeper healing. Confrontation is a very specific skill in ministry. We might have more freedom to confront those we are in relationship with. A friend might be able to hear you; a stranger might tell you to buzz off.

In ministry, seekers are looking for help, not advice. If we respond quickly with advice, they might shut down and may not look for help again for a long time. As a *helper,* we earn the right to speak into their life only when we have heard what they have to say by listening to understand. Some might begin talking and won't stop to take a breath for forty-five minutes. The time we take to listen and truly hear their story is a significant way we show them their value. Our listening skills can validate their feelings and show them we truly care.

At some point during the time we spend with individuals, there may come a time that we as helpers see a need for *gentle confrontation.* We use tentative statements and ask questions that seekers can consider before making a choice to let go of those things that are keeping them in bondage. We ask questions like "Is it possible you have not forgiven your mother for the things she said to you?" and "Is it possible you dishonored your mother and father during your time of rebellion?"

And sometimes the question might take a form like "It sounds as if the words you have been saying to yourself are not very encouraging. In fact, they may have the power of a curse. Would you like to pray and ask God to forgive you for thinking and believing these things and renounce the curse you have put on yourself?" We only know to ask these questions when we have heard enough of their story to understand what needs to be addressed. We may even hear some things they did not share if we listen closely enough to the story they are sharing with us.

Many years ago, I was listening to a woman share her story about the abuse she suffered from her mother and how damaging that was for her. She said that she "hated" her mother. I led her through forgiveness for the hurts she had described. Then, because she used the word *hate*, I just couldn't move on without addressing it. I asked if she could possibly ask God to forgive her for the "spirit of murder." She immediately responded, "How did you know?" She then confessed having an abortion as a young adult. She did ask God to forgive her for the abortion and the spirit of murder.

The Bible tells us: "Whoever hates his brother is a murderer, and you know that no murderer has eternal life abiding in him" (1 John 3:15). In my experience with ministry, it is rare that an evil spirit will leave a person unless it is confronted. My question about the spirit was related to her mother, but God used it to help her get into another area that needed healing.

An extensive ministry time will consist of a series of *gentle confrontations* to lead the seeker to freedom.

Control

Who is in control? The *seeker*. The *helper* offers suggestions, not commands or advice. Give seekers time to evaluate what you are suggesting, and then allow them the opportunity to agree, disagree, or request further explanation.

Often, in the process of forgiveness, it takes time for them to evaluate exactly what it is they're giving up. I prefer to watch them process without interruption, while they count the cost of what the offender owes them. When they are given this opportunity, they realize that when they forgive, they are eliminating the debt. Sometimes this will take more than a single day. It's okay if they are not ready to deal with all this debt at the time. I pray with them for God's grace to help them. Sometimes, when I ask if they would like to pray for God's grace, they are not ready to take that step, or they don't believe that what I'm suggesting applies to them, and that's fine. The helper may be one hundred percent correct, but if *seekers* don't understand the connection just then, let it pass, and God will reveal it to them at another time. We want to meet them where they are. When they are ready to take that step and follow through, we might meet with them two or three more times.

THE SETTING

Some seekers will be uncomfortable with the ministry setting for various reasons. Years ago, we were ministering to a class of thirty students in Chile when a situation like this arose. There was a young woman who had experienced physical abuse from her father. When it was her turn for ministry she sat down between me and Carla, her body language screamed that she was uncomfortable with the arrangement of the ministry setting. I asked her if she would be more comfortable with me sitting somewhere else. "Yes," she said immediately. "I want you sitting over there where I can see you." I asked one of the other female helpers to take my place, and I moved to the other side of the room.

An interesting process often takes place in a healing ministry of this nature. Many times, in one of these healing moments, although it was a man who inflicted the wounding to the female, a man will also be used as part of the healing process. And there will also be times when a woman can be part of the healing process when a man has been wounded by a female. The most important thing to keep in mind is this: the helper is not in control. Actually, the order of persons in control goes as follows: first, God; second, the *seeker*; and third, the helper. We must be careful not to quench either the Spirit of God or the spirit of the seeker.

When we come to a stopping place in ministry, or if they have prayed through everything the Lord has shown them, many will ask, "What next?" The truth is, there is always a next step.

Next Steps

Whether we meet with a person only once or several times, there is always a next step. What can they do to continue on the journey they've begun or even move beyond it? The ability to coach the seeker toward the next step can be as important as the ministry itself. Walking in the freedom of the Spirit is a process; healing is a process; life is a process. We may continue to struggle in relationships after we've been through a significant time of ministry.

Tom Marshall's book *Right Relationships* is very beneficial in helping us set healthy boundaries, even in relationships with relatives. Another helpful book is *Boundaries*, written by Henry Cloud and John Townsend.

Some we have worked with go into "Life Coaching". Some seek a Life Coach while others become a Life Coach.

Many seekers come to our ministry from a twelve-step group. It is quite possible these people will need to return to such a group for continued support. God's Word tells us the devil will try to steal the blessings we've received.

Some will need a new group of friends, a change in environment, or a change in lifestyle. A small group or mentor could be invaluable to seekers as they continue their journey.

And never forget the foundation of our new life: God's Word. It is always a good idea to get into a Bible study and begin applying the truth of God's Word in our lives.

Beyond the healing process, there is also a need for those who have received a measure of healing to have a place in ministry themselves. Sometimes the next step is asking what I can do for others. What is the Lord putting on your heart in regard to furthering His kingdom? Helping others will be the next step for some. This is when I tell those who have done so well "God loves you and I have a plan for your life".

CHAPTER 5

Ministry Models

This section is intended to give helpers a guide or method of ministry for various situations. During our time in missions, my wife and I learned that in order to be effective in sharing the gospel, we needed to understand the culture we were trying to reach. To do this, we had to spend time in that culture. We had to learn more than just people's language; we needed to learn their traditions, their beliefs, and their worldview. We needed to be students of the very people we were going to mentor.

Please consider how this is also true when doing ministry. Try seeing the life experience of those you are doing ministry with as though you are entering into their culture for a period of time. Each ministry type is similar to identifying with a different culture. In order to help someone through healing of the life experiences they've endured, it is necessary to identify with them. A key need for anyone seeking help is to be understood. Not only do we want to identify with them, but we want to empathize with them as well.

We would like to have a keen understanding—or at least a basic knowledge—of what life was like in their home and even what life must have been like at various stages of their lives. Some might believe that we need to have lived through the same life experiences as a seeker in order to be effective, but this is not the case. I have personally ministered to seekers from dozens of ethnic backgrounds and lifestyles and have not experienced any of their hardships. We learn what they need by listening to them tell their stories and having compassion for them. God will use us as vessels to heal those who come from the "fourth world" (the world of the abused).

With every seeker who comes for help I default to one basic. I ask them to do a personal inventory of their past so we can begin helping in a healthier place. I do this regardless of the current problem they are seeking help for. I have a personal ministry book I give them that describes the possible bondages they may have been dealing with and I ask them to complete the ministry sheet in the booklet before we try to address present day issues. When working with couples in conflict, I can't even help them be nice to one another until hurts of the past have been healed.

You may download the booklet Handbook to Healing, free on my website, www.healingbeyondcounseling.com . This along with several free resources will be available for reference to different ministry models shared about in this book.

Specific Ministry Models

1. **Help Them Forgive**

2. **Rejection**

3. **Abandonment**

4. **Relationship Conflict**

5. **Control**

6. **Adult Children of Alcoholics**

7. **Adult Children of Divorce**

8. **Miscarriage/Stillbirth**

9. **Abortion**

10. **Breaking Soul Ties**

11. **Inappropriate Authority**

12. **Sexual Abuse, Molestation, or Incest**

13. **Domestic Violence**

14. **Unwed or Single Mothers**

15. **Addictions**

16. **Identificational Repentance**

17. **Performance Orientation**

18. **Suicide**

19. **Father/Mother Heart Ministry**

20. **Ministry Preparation**

Helpful Do's for Effective Ministry

- **Pray** before ministry time and at the beginning of a ministry session.
- **Prevent** the possibility of distractions. When you are ministering in a home, pets or children can be an unneeded interruption.
- **Help** seekers feel they are in control. Avoid directive or imperative statements, such as *you should* or *you need to*. Only pursue what they are willing to address.
- **Partner** with another helper when doing ministry with a seeker of the opposite sex. This shows respect for the seeker and is a protection for you as a minister.
- Following the initial emotional purge, try to **pray** as you go. Some seekers may begin to share extremely long stories and complicated interactions with various family members. Try to pray as you go over issues as they are being described.
- **Father Heart** Ministry (detailed later in this section) may be needed during an emotional purge and to close a ministry session or series of ministry sessions.
- **Listen** for and identify the spiritual bondage to pray about.
- **Effective** – You will be more effective if you help them pray for their own choices.
- **Encourage** them to pray aloud, and help them by leading them if necessary.

- **Suggest** – Give instructions as suggestions: "Is it possible?" or "It could be helpful …."
- **Describe** the particular step of redemption to apply, and coach them through the prayer.
- **Remain** in view in front of the person throughout the ministry time. Trust is an integral factor in ministry, and some will want to have you in full view at all times.
- **Keep** your eyes open when you are ministering prayer. You might miss what the Lord is doing with a person if you are not aware of their body language.
- **Confront** an evil spirit in order to make it flee. If you suspect an unclean spirit, ask the seeker if this is a possibility, and if it is, inquire about the seeker's willingness to renounce the intruder.
- **Specific** – Help them be specific when they forgive. The more specific they can be, the more healing they will experience.
- **Silence** is your ally. The Holy Spirit is working in those times of silence. Just wait.
- **When repenting,** call the sin for what it is. If we downplay, or try to make what has been done less than it was, they won't experience freedom.
- **Keep** your advice. Share a brief testimony instead: "A similar event happened in my life, and the Lord met me in this way when I …."
- **Save** preaching for Sunday. If you need to preach, you're the one needing help.
- **Ask** for the Holy Spirit to fill them while praying the closing prayer. When spiritual ground has been taken from the enemy, it is important to ask the Holy Spirit to come and fill the person.
- **Seal** the work done in this ministry time with prayer so the enemy can't steal back any ground that has been gained.

Help Them Forgive

The first thing to address, with nearly every bondage, is forgiveness. It is most important that every seeker understand the necessity of forgiveness. We really don't have authority to break a curse, inappropriate authority, judgment, or soul ties until forgiveness has taken place. Repentance is also necessary in order to break some bondages. Unforgiveness is an open door that allows the enemy to come into our lives and take up residence. Unforgiveness turns into resentment, and resentment turns into bitterness. Such a person is then handed over to the tormentors, as Jesus describes in the book of Matthew.

THE PROBLEM

Many are in so much pain, they have a difficult time even approaching the thought of forgiveness. The hurt is so deep that they cannot see how forgiveness is going to help. The more unthinkable the offense, the more difficult it may be for them to embrace the thought of forgiving their offender. The challenge for the helper is getting the seeker to see the only way to their freedom is in forgiveness.

We are most helpful when we allow seekers an opportunity to share long enough for us to get an accurate description of the many offenses contained within the larger offense. Then we can help them be specific when they do begin to forgive. I try to explain that this thing called forgiveness is not easy, and in our own humanness we aren't able to forgive. We must receive God's grace in order to do this. Some offenses have had such an impact on us, and have had such a hold on us for so long, we need strength from the Lord in order to forgive.

If seekers pray earnestly for this grace, this grace will be given to them. I have seen this grace come instantly, and then I have seen it take weeks to be received. I have ministered to some in so much pain at the time they had no strength to pray themselves. At such times I will pray for them, asking that they receive the grace necessary to begin.

When seekers share the essence of their wounds, they are also given the opportunity to assess the amount of the debt they are about to give up. This process is similar to giving them a ledger sheet to begin listing what they are owed by the person who hurt them. When they are able to pray through every offense on the sheet, the balance of the debt is zero.

Relational Wounds

Some will come with relational conflicts involving spouses or family members. These wounds are often difficult to forgive. I have dealt with some people in these circumstances who have never forgiven anyone—let alone family members—in their lives. These people might need to begin by asking the Holy Spirit to show them who the first person was who ever hurt them, and start there. Continue chronologically to the current offense if necessary.

I once ministered to a man who shared about several family members who had been very abusive, both physically and verbally, when he was a child and into his teen years. After he had finished sharing about these traumatic events from the past, I asked him who he might be able to forgive. He could not forgive anyone. I asked if he could forgive any of his ex-wives. He could not.

Finally, I asked him to give me one person he could forgive. "This is the only way I can help you," I said. "I don't care who it is; let's start there." He began by forgiving his current wife. We finally did get to his most recent ex-wife and other significant people to release. Eventually, we helped him begin asking God's forgiveness for the horrible things he had done to others and then to begin forgiving himself.

No Excuses

Don't let the seeker excuse the wounding behavior of an authority figure. "I know they did the best they could" and "They were wounded too" are examples of reasoning the hurt away as an adult. Sometimes it is easier for us to deny than it is to accept, but we need to address the hurt we felt as a child. When we excuse the behavior, we reduce what it is we are forgiving, and we are denying our own pain. Challenge the Seeker to forgive as if the offender did the action on purpose. Adults will tend to deal with abuse from their childhoods on a cognitive level. When they can deal with the abuse on a spiritual and emotional level, they will be free! If the adult appears emotionally disconnected, try praying for the Holy Spirit to reveal the feelings stirred up by the offenses. The adult may have made a vow not to cry anymore or never to be hurt again, possibly taking control or even denying the feelings. Ask them to trust God to be in control of their feelings.

When seekers tell you they have forgiven someone, consider asking them one or more of the following questions:

- What did you forgive them for? (Is it general or specific?)
- What do they owe you?
- Are you willing to say, *"I forgive them and they owe me nothing, and/or I forgive them and ask God to bless them"* (This last prayer is a new level of forgiveness that brings great peace).

Revenge or Justice

The desire for revenge or justice is a common block to forgiveness. The right to revenge and justice must be relinquished.

Stuck in the Past

Explain to the Seeker that although they may feel they deserved something different than the life they experienced, they didn't get it. They can't change the past, and the loss is still causing them heartache. Walk them through giving up the right to have what they deserved (childhood, virginity, etc.).

God Is the Parent

Seekers can ask God to heal the hole in their heart. They can ask God to restore them and to re-parent them.

Daily Offences

When offenses occur daily, forgiveness may be a lifestyle, or healthy boundaries may be needed. Encourage the seeker to learn about healthy boundaries.

Reconciliation

Seekers may need to ask their parents, spouse, or children, for forgiveness. They also may need to ask a representative of the body of Christ Forgiveness as well for the freedom from shame to be complete.

Forgiveness Is Ultimately between You and the Lord

When you forgive others, you do not need to tell them you did so. Please do not go to Mom and Dad and tell them, "I forgave you for all the horrible things you did to me as a child." Forgiveness is not about who the "bigger person" is; it is an act of obedience to the Lord.

How the Seeker prays matters: "I forgive ..." or "I choose to forgive ..." instead of "Lord, help me forgive ...," "I want to forgive ...," or "I'd like to forgive ...."

Rejection

Rejection is the most common wound experienced in the world we live in. We can experience rejection at home, at school, or in the workplace. It is difficult to go through life without experiencing some form of rejection.

Not only is rejection the most common emotional wound, but it can also be the most damaging. Rejection can affect our belief system and cause us to have a negative core belief about ourselves. We are learning that a sense of rejection can even begin in the womb. This has the potential to affect many areas in a person's life. Some who have been rejected by authority figures in their lives may even reject themselves, which is a painful place in life.

We have prayed with many people who struggle with wounds of rejection. Sometimes I will open a cabinet door in my office where a mirror hangs. I ask the seeker to stand in front of the mirror. While seekers stand there, I ask them to seek forgiveness for rejecting themselves and gently attempt to help them accept themselves. Some will resist this with surprising zeal. One woman asked if she could leave and work on this exercise at home. She did work on it at home, and the Lord worked a miracle in her life. She had been stuck for years. This is her story:

How I Accepted Myself

I wanted you to know that I wasn't avoiding you or my "mirror ministry." I am still working on being comfortable looking at myself. Some moments are easier than others. But I want you to know that "rejecting myself" was truly a revelation for me. I realize now that this is what I was unable to identify. I am getting freedom! Isn't the Holy Spirit awesome? Thank you so much, Gary!

I felt instructed to write a letter to myself. So I did. I am sending it to you. If the Holy Spirit reveals anything to you, please let me know.

Dearest and Beloved Child of God,

I come remorsefully to you. I have wronged you as a person and as a treasured child of God. God called you beautiful, and I called you hideous. I am so very sorry. You are truly beautiful inside. But you are beautiful on the outside too. Do you hear me? You are beautiful on the outside! The color of your eyes is stunning. Your smile is radiant. Your dimples are adorable. Your hair is soft, and the color is beautiful. Your hands are elegant. Your figure is shapely and attractive.

I am sorry that I have trapped you into a false belief about yourself by forcing you to dwell on your perceived imperfections: cellulite, weight, wrinkles, brow, chest, butt, and feet. I have heaped torment on you by attacking your mind. I have told you that you are not intelligent. I have told you that you can't remember anything. I have told you that you are incapable of starting and participating in meaningful conversations.

These are all lies, Carol. Do you hear me? I have cursed you. And now in the name of Jesus, I am breaking those curses. We are taking back the ground we have given the devil by believing those lies.

And Father God, I ask You to forgive me. I choose to believe You, Lord. I choose to forgive myself for believing all those lies. Believing the lies came with a mighty high price tag. It has robbed me and my family and my friends. It has robbed people I don't even know because the lies rendered me useless. How could God use me to reach other people when I have been paralyzed and tormented in my mind?

I thank You, Father, for Your Son, Jesus. Without Jesus I would never have freedom. I am delivered from the power of darkness and brought into God's kingdom. I am set free, victorious, and blessed. I am created in God's image, and I am being changed into the likeness of Jesus. I am a new person. I have the mind and attitude of Christ. I have the peace of God which is beyond all understanding. I can do all things through Christ, who strengthens me.

God said, "You are beautifully and wonderfully made," and He is right! I have lied to you. And I am deeply remorseful for doing so. I have watched you go from sweet innocence to deep despair from all the lies I have told you. I have robbed you and your family of joy and peace. I have robbed you from operating in the fruits of the Spirit; love, joy, peace, patience, kindness, goodness, faithfulness, gentleness, and self-control.

These lies have been insidious! They are torment and they are death. They have caused me to neglect myself and to neglect others. They have caused me to harden my heart.

Dear Lord, I am so very sorry. I ask Your forgiveness again for believing the lies, which have not only rendered me useless but also caused me to strike out at others in my anguish and my pain. I have rejected others because of my own self-rejection. And I have also rejected You, Lord, when the lies were louder than Your voice. Lord, I pray Your voice becomes so loud that I am not able to dwell anywhere else.

I am chosen, and I am God's masterpiece. I am created in Christ Jesus for good works.

Much love,
Myself, God's most precious possession and
the apple of His eye ~ Carol

Praying through Rejection

When doing a spiritual inventory, we usually identify the big rocks to discard during the initial ministry session. It may take a few more sessions to identify all the instances when a person has experienced wounds of rejection. As we identify such instances, it is helpful to recognize that some rejection can be subtle and not easily identified. Pray through and lead seekers to forgive each offense of both obvious and subtle rejection. After completing ministry that addresses the incidents in their inventory, pray for them to receive a spirit of acceptance.

REJECTION IN THE WOMB

It is possible to pray through a comprehensive list of rejections in a seeker's life and not see a noticeable change in the person. When ministry is effective, you will usually see some kind of physical change come over a person. It usually looks like a slow-motion reel of them coming to life or a time-lapse video of a flower blooming.

If there is no apparent change at the end of an entire ministry session, I suspect rejection in the womb. You might ask what they know about their conception. Some have survived an attempted abortion. Some have had parents or grandparents suggest abortion. Others were abandoned by their father either before they were born or soon after. Whatever the circumstance, lead seekers to forgive and renounce the rejection/abandonment. Do Father heart ministry (explained later). Pray for them to receive God as their Father.

Abandonment

The ultimate rejection, abandonment is like telling children they should not have been born. This kind of wounding can remain with a person well into the adult years. It directly affects how people function in relationships. They might become possessive or controlling in adult relationships or have extreme anxiety because they fear someone they are close to may reject them.

Identifying the abandonment they have suffered could help them find healing of their wound. In today's families, some adults think it is normal to come from a single-parent home or a stepfamily. They don't recognize Dad leaving them when they were young as abandonment. It has become more and more the norm for a child to be raised either in a single-parent home or to be raised by grandparents. Help them pray and forgive the abandonment and renounce the rejection. Again, you can do Father heart ministry in this area of void and neglect.

Relationship Conflict

It is rare that someone comes into my office for something other than some kind of relationship conflict. The conflict is either with others, God, or themselves. Gary Smalley says it best in his book *DNA of Relationships*: "Life is all about relationships. Everything else is just details." Another great quote on relationships is from author Les Parrot: "Until you have gone through the hard work of getting yourself emotionally whole, all your future relationships will fall hopelessly flat." My wife and I have been involved in the healing ministry for over twenty years now, and we have found these two statements to be absolutely true. We have found that in any relationship, we must go through the hurts and regrets of the past in order to help people function well in their present relationships.

HOW DO YOU RESOLVE CONFLICT?

The following principles apply to all relationships.

When a couple comes to me because their relationship is in trouble, it becomes apparent during the first visit that they need a healthy model for resolving conflict. Often the first question I ask is "Could you give me an example of how you resolve conflict?"

Even people who were raised in church often lack a healthy example of conflict resolution. As a result, many couples have never really resolved any conflict or offense in their relationship. A common response to my question is along these lines: "Whatever happened, we ignored it and went on with our lives." This method of conflict resolution, however, only creates division. Many of these couples experienced a division while they were in the dating period and essentially began their marriage already divided.

When we get up the next day after a hurt or offense has been ignored, and carry on as if nothing happened, the unresolved conflict lies like an elephant under the rug. This begins the breakdown of the relationship. Unresolved conflict causes one or both of the partners to begin closing their spirit off to each other, and the two never really become one. Trust is damaged, or a measure of respect is lost as a result of unresolved conflict.

THE FIRST OFFENSE

The second thing I ask during the first interview is for one of them to describe the first unresolved conflict or offense in their relationship, so I can understand what it looked like. I have learned from working with many couples that the breakdown of their relationship began with the first unresolved conflict. Sometimes both partners have carried an offense away from the same event. It is likely that each partner has a different perception of what took place during the event.

THE BAT AND THE TELEVISION

A woman shared the following story with me: One day after work, she and her husband began to argue, and he became very angry. He was so angry he took a baseball bat and broke the television screen. When he woke up the next morning, he acted as if nothing had happened and asked his wife what they were having for breakfast.

Clearly, the husband had no grid for resolving conflict. Without exception, it is critical to identify the offense, take responsibility for our part in the matter, and ask forgiveness. This is necessary for reconciliation in a relationship.

Conflict Resolution

Many couples tell me they can't remember the first offense. After visiting with them for a while, I usually find that one of them remembers the offense and remembers it well. If, indeed, neither of them remembers the first offense, I suggest that we ask the Holy Spirit to help us. If they can't remember after we pray, I ask them to share events they do remember. One of them will remember the first event the next time we meet.

Sometimes, one of the spouses will begin to share the initial offense, only to have the other spouse interrupt them to say, "No, that wasn't the first offense; let me tell you what the first offense was." When the offense has been identified, I then model what conflict resolution can look like. "I'm sorry what I did was wrong. I sinned against in this way…(cheated, lied, and deceived) would you forgive me?"

After one of the spouses shares an offense committed by the other, I ask them to elaborate and give specifics, describing their feelings and how they were affected at the time, so their partner knows what to ask forgiveness for. Then I ask one or both of them to acknowledge their part in the offense. Often, if one partner has been offended, the other is not aware of the offense. Once we have resolved the first offenses, the couple is able to see where the relationship began to break down. Many times, married couples identify the first unresolved hurt or conflict and realize it happened before they were married. With some couples, the unresolved conflict even happened on their wedding day or shortly thereafter.

PREMARITAL SEX MAY BE THE FIRST OFFENSE

Premarital sex can be the first offense with those who are raised in Christian homes or homes with high moral standards, and these marriages can experience trouble in later years. Some were pregnant when they got married, and as a result, the marriage began with a sense of shame for one or both of them. The guilt and shame cause a conflict for one or both partners. The couple may go for several years experiencing numerous conflicts, and one or both may become disrespectful toward the other.

Both partners need healing from the sin of dishonoring their parents and dishonoring each other. This is not easily recognized by the couple, and in this case, finding the problem is like looking for a needle in a haystack. The relationship can be restored when the partners ask forgiveness for dishonoring each other. The next step is asking God to forgive them for dishonoring their mother and father and for dishonoring the body of Christ. I suggest they also go to their parents and ask forgiveness for the dishonor (this, of course, depends on the values in the family of origin for each one). If either is struggling with shame, they may also need to forgive themselves.

HUMILITY AND FORGIVENESS

No relationship will endure without humility and forgiveness. Pride is one of the major challenges to overcome before reconciliation can occur. If both refuse to take responsibility for their actions or admit their own part in an offense, resolution is almost impossible. This is especially true with our children. If a parent can acknowledge her or his mistake and ask forgiveness, the respect previously lost can be regained. This is even more essential with stepchildren. If parents continue on as if they had every right to act in the manner that caused the offense, they soon lose the respect of those they are close to.

When reflecting upon myself and my behavior at the age of forty-six, I finally realized I needed to take responsibility for certain actions. One by one, I went to my wife, my parents, my in-laws, and my children to resolve the effects of my behavior toward them. I still have to humble myself with those I may have hurt by acknowledging how my actions were inconsiderate or hurtful.

The Importance of Forgiveness

Simply stated, no relationship can either be reconciled or grow without forgiveness. When I hear seekers say, "I find it hard to forgive," I suspect they have never really forgiven anyone. How can any relationship continue without forgiveness? In order to help those in this place, I suggest to them that we go back to the first time they remember being hurt, rejected, or offended. Here I can begin coaching them through forgiveness.

One way to approach this is by asking a few basic questions about the conflict that brought them to us: "What happened?" "Can you describe your behavior in the incident?" "How did you feel?" and "What did you believe?" When I have these answers, I then ask, "When in your life have you felt like this or believed this way before?" Most often, this will take a person back to a childhood event. Their answer, which is often immediate, is usually something like "I felt and believed this since I was nine years old when Mom/Dad said to me …." Now we are getting to the root.

Remember, "The problem is never the problem." When we can walk someone through forgiving a childhood event, they will begin recognizing the freedom that comes with it. Forgiving current offenses in their lives now will become much easier.

A Closed Spirit

I usually ask if at some point one or the other chose to close off their spirit to the other (another principle I borrowed from Gary Smalley in one of his first videos). Many acknowledge they have. When this is confessed, I include this in the resolution process. Seekers not only take responsibility for what they've done to offend the other but also ask forgiveness for closing their spirit off. Then they can pray, choosing to open their spirit to their partner. Please recognize this can be a risk to open your spirit to someone who has hurt you in the past. However If one continues to have walls of protection in the relationship they will continue to be divided.

I have worked with countless couples, one or both of whom have closed their spirits off to their spouse. This can happen early in the relationship due to an unresolved offense from years before. Some of these couples persevere for years before trying to get help. Many of them have been to counselors, trying to work on communication skills, personality differences, and a host of other issues, only to quit counseling, frustrated and hopeless.

Many have also shared stories with me explaining how something that happened to them as a child or teen caused them to close off to one of their parents. They had harbored an offense in their heart for years, and some of the parents simply thought their teen was just going through a phase of rebellion. To redeem this behavior, I ask the person if they are willing to pray and forgive the offense, and then ask God to forgive the closing off of their spirit. I then suggest they ask forgiveness from the one against whom they closed their spirit off. The next step is to pray and choose to open their spirit.

Some have even closed off to anyone who tries getting close to them. If this is the case, I often help them identify vows made in this regard, such as "I'll never let anyone get close to me again." "I'll never trust," or "I'll never be hurt again."

ADULTERY, A NEW BEGINNING

Adultery is devastating to a relationship. It takes work and time to get through the pain of this offense, but it can actually strengthen a relationship if both people are willing to work through it. The initial challenge is to help the offended spouse understand that the action is only a symptom of a relational problem that has existed for some time. One of the shortcomings of being human is that we seldom seek to correct an issue in a healthy way until we are in crisis. Many times, our attempt in the flesh to correct a failing relationship only causes more problems. Eventually, after many failures, we look toward the One who can help us in the correct way: Jesus Christ.

WOUNDS OF BETRAYAL

A person who has been betrayed often finds it impossible to see the whole picture and is unable to do anything other than blame the other for all the pain that has been caused. Of course, I allow the offended person to talk about what happened and how wrong it was, and I suggest that eventually it will be necessary to begin working through forgiveness. During the process, if the victim continues to look at their partner as the sole source of the problem, I might ask, "Do you really believe you had no fault in this?" With both spouses present, I ask the offending spouse to acknowledge what they have done and repent to God. The next step is for them to ask their spouse for forgiveness and to ask the body of Christ for forgiveness as well. I qualify to the offended spouse that I don't expect them to forgive immediately, but I encourage them to ask God for the grace to begin forgiving. With the spouse present, I ask the one who has had the affair to follow me in breaking soul ties with the person they had the sinful relationship with.

DIVERT THE SESSION

I have found that, because of the intense emotion around the current offense, it is often better to avoid the present-day problem and ask them to help me understand the first offense in their relationship. This helps take the focus off the new offense. When the first offense is identified and we begin walking them through the resolution of that event, other unresolved conflicts may come to the surface as well. This process helps them understand how the relationship broke down long before the adultery occurred. Many times, the offended spouse will see their role in the initial breakdown. This understanding can begin the confession and forgiveness of different offenses through the years of their relationship. When these past offenses have been identified, the couple can begin to see how events in the past have led them to the current offense. It is like a domino effect when the first offence is identified. Subsequent offences through the years begin falling like stacked dominos. Now the current affair seems of little importance.

In several cases, the offended spouse actually becomes grateful for the affair, because it causes them to work on their relationship in a way they never had before. The level of intimacy and love for one another can become greater than it has ever been up to that point.

THE EXCEPTION

When sexual addiction is the real cause of adultery, I take a completely different approach toward resolution. If addiction is evident, the problem or breakdown began long before the couple ever became an exclusive couple. In this case, the offended partner truly is the victim, and I try to get the partner into a support group for the spouses of sex addicts.

If the addict really wants to save the marriage, I recommend a twelve-step program, and I encourage professional intervention. I recommend a therapist who specializes in attachment disorders. I also recommend the couple go to an intensive workshop designed specifically for dealing with sexual addictions. This involves the addict working through complete disclosure and confirmation of the disclosure with a lie detector test. A professional counselor helps the couple through some therapy, setting up accountability and periodic lie detector tests for the protection of the spouse. Group therapy may also be an option.

SEPARATION? MAYBE

There may be the need for a temporary separation, blood test, and lie detector test before the addict is allowed to live in the home or sleep in the same bed. After an agreed time of separation, the addict can move back into the home. This is only recommended after progress is proven by passing a lie detector test, usually after three months. There are a number of books and ministries explaining the details of this addiction and the work involved for both spouses to reconcile the relationship. We have been using these methods for several years with couples in our church, experiencing great success and saving marriages.

If the addict does not have a heart of repentance or will not submit to the process suggested, which includes a twelve-step program, lie detector test, family of origin work, and professional intervention, I have little hope for the marriage. Often, addicts will determine they can do this on their own and they don't need any of the above. In this case, they have set themselves up for failure. Even if addicts have acknowledged all they have done, if there is not repentance and brokenness, change will not happen.

To Reconcile a Relationship

Without exception, I encourage both partners to do some family-of-origin work. I don't attempt to help them with communication skills or suggest changes in behavior until both partners have gone through what I call a spiritual inventory. This process gives them the opportunity to clean up the hurts and regrets of their past. I want to give them the opportunity to apply the redemption of the cross to every area of their lives. I don't expect them to even have the desire or ability to nurture one another until some work on their past has been accomplished.

Control

A common conflict in relationships revolves around the issue of control. One person tries to control the other. Dozens of times, during after-service prayer at church, mothers have come forward asking us to pray for their adult child who is "acting out." The child, they say, is involved in drugs, alcohol, inappropriate relationships, or all three. Many times, there is a controlling parent in families where this issue exists.

If we take time to hear the rest of the story, we'll find the parent has taken responsibility for the adult child's behavior, which includes years of enabling and controlling. This began when the child was a teen or even younger. In this type of relationship, the parent consistently rescues the child, bails her or him out of jail, and supplies money that the child uses to further the self-destructive behavior. The well-intentioned parent will rescue the child from the consequences of his or her actions over and over before recognizing that such "help" is no help at all. Let God have control. He is more capable than we are.

A controlling parent is often the root cause behind a child with an eating disorder. And the "acting out" the parent complains about might be the child's way of escaping from the control. In these instances, the only time I see change come is when parents relinquish the child to the Lord. By doing this, they say they will allow their children to experience the consequences of their behavior. A parent's only responsibility is to wait for adult children to want help and look for it themselves.

Most adult children of alcoholics have issues with the need for control. The root of their need to control may vary from abandonment issues to their lives being out of control when they were children. It helps to identify vows concerning control and then to pray and break free from them. I also suggest they address the traumatic events in their past one at a time, pray through each one, and release the right to be in control of each event by giving it back to God. Seldom will a seeker take me up on that suggestion. Why? I don't know.

THE ROOT OF CONTROL

Unbelief is the root cause of controlling behavior. This is a common occurrence with a parent who has an adult child who is consistently in trouble. The parent enables and rescues the child, preventing God from working in the child's life by allowing her or him to experience the natural (or legal) consequences of the behavior. These parents are not trusting that God is in control. They are attempting to fix the situation themselves. If these parents can't trust God, ask them why. If they decide they are ready to trust Him, lead them in a prayer of repentance and relinquishment.

Adult Child of Alcoholics

Performance orientation is probably the most common consequence of an alcoholic home. The most common ministry model to learn would be to know what life experiences a child might have had living in an alcoholic home. If you do not have knowledge of this kind of home, there are many books telling the stories of what home life there is like. We have learned about this culture by simply listening to different people share their stories.

THE MINEFIELD

The most common traumatic event for children in alcoholic homes is the continuing atmosphere of living in a minefield. They never know when the next blowup will occur, when the outburst of anger is coming, or when someone is going to be hit. They don't know what they've done wrong or what they failed to do. No one knows when the hammer will fall, and they don't know why. They only know that sooner or later the pin will be pulled out of the grenade and an explosion will follow. They walk on eggshells and even take responsibility for how one parent's anger may be taken out on the other.

SIBLING OR PARENT?

The older siblings may take on the responsibility for raising the younger siblings and doing most of the chores around the house. Some assume the responsibility, and others are made to take the responsibility. The older sibling makes breakfast for the younger children before school and sees that the laundry is done for the day. Sometimes, the older sibling assumes responsibility for changing the baby's diapers, because the parents are either absent or unable to function. These child-parents often become leaders and overachievers. They will become very good at what they do if they have not adopted their parents' behavior and become alcoholics or drug addicts themselves. Either way a large portion of the child's childhood is lost.

THEY LIVE WITH SHAME

Many children of alcoholics are not allowed to have friends over to their house. Others will not risk doing so, because of the embarrassment. Many of these children have never had birthday parties, they've never had friends sleep over, and they've never invited others over for dinner. In one of our discipleship schools, a young man twenty-eight years old had his first birthday party. The children learn to lie about why their parents don't ever come to school functions like parent–teacher conferences or school plays. By the time they are adults, lying in order to spare the family embarrassment has become second nature to the point they lie even when they don't need to.

Poverty and Fear

Poverty is common in the alcoholic home. The selfishness of the addict often steals food, proper clothing, and medical attention from the family. Fear hangs over the home like a never-ending fog. The children seldom feel safe.

Many times, the children are awakened in the night because the parents are fighting. Often, the fighting becomes physical, which frightens the children even more. One young man shared with us that his mother and father fought viciously when he was a child. One night, when the boy was only eight years old, the parents were fighting so violently that he wet the bed because he was too afraid to get up and go to the bathroom. Another man shared how he would hide his younger siblings under his bed when the fighting would start.

Abandonment Is Common

Abandonment by one parent or the other is common. Some adult children don't recognize the abandonment if both parents stayed in the home. There is always abandonment, whether it is physical or emotional. Some alcoholics are not "mean drunks"; they are emotionally numb, so they too have abandoned the family.

Need for Control

Children of alcoholics will have strong tendencies to need control in their adult life. They grew up in an environment of chaos and complete absence of control, so naturally, they overcompensate as adults and have a very strong need to feel they are in control of all situations and relationships, attempting to maintain harmony at all cost. This reaction is often enforced in their adult life by vows made during these chaotic times.

Vows

"I'll never be a drunk like my mom." "I'll never marry an alcoholic." These are possible vows and judgments some might make. Even if they never take a drink themselves, most will fall into some compulsive behavior such as eating disorders, workaholism, exercise, perfectionism, and so on. This is how they will attempt to cope with the emotional pain they carry. Many will end up being drinkers themselves, and the shame of breaking their vow will keep them stuck in the addiction.

Adult Children of Divorce

Often, children will think something is wrong with them and believe they are the reason Mom or Dad left. Even in the best cases of divorce, the father is not always there when he is needed. In some relationships, the mother can be so difficult to deal with that Dad finds another woman—who has her own children—adopts that family, and perhaps then abandons or has little to do with his own children. The prospect of dealing with the angry ex-wife deters him from visiting his own kids. I have seen cases where the father bought expensive gifts for his stepchildren but gave nothing to his biological children.

It is easy for the biological children to feel envy and bitterness toward the stepchildren and to desire their own rights. I have often prayed with seekers in their forties who are still angry at the stepchildren for taking their dad away. Sometimes, the stepmother manipulates the father so that it isn't safe for him to show affection to his own kids without experiencing consequences at home.

Feeling Unwanted

One woman shared that her husband left because he didn't want five children. The youngest daughter heard this stated more than once. When ministry time came for the youngest daughter, she questioned whether she should have ever been born. In cases like this, I suspect rejection in the womb to be a strong possibility also.

A Complicated Life

Consider the possibilities of life for children after divorce. Most are living in a single-parent home or a stepfamily. Life is never going to be the same as they once knew it. They may need to change schools. Holidays are split between families. The number of relatives may even double, which means the number of relationships also doubles. Every other weekend involves packing a backpack to visit dad, sometimes in another town. They need clothes at both houses. Financial strain is almost certain, which means the same luxuries are no longer an option. Siblings may even be separated. Who is Dad's new girlfriend? How many? The complications go on, some of which are continuous.

Rejection in the Womb

Wounds of rejection and abandonment can be devastating. When seekers begin forgiving, the pain often causes an emotional response. Often the pain is so deep they are not able to begin communicating and sharing what happened. The Bible instructs us to lay hands on people sometimes when we pray for them. I have found the laying on of hands can be effective in cases like these. I will hold them and begin praying for the Lord to comfort them and flood them with peace. When they have calmed, I will ask if they can begin sharing their story. Many describe how Dad left when they were two years old or younger. When abandonment happens at such a young age, I suspect rejection in the womb as well. If you've prayed about all the rejections in a seeker's life but still see no significant change in the person's countenance, try praying for the rejection in the womb. When doing this ministry with my wife or another woman helper I ask the seeker to sit on her lap as we pray for them. My wife has ministered to men in their fifties in this way and we see God's mother heart ministered in this way.

Poverty

The financial state of the family will change even with the well-to-do. With some, the father does not continue with child support, making provision for the children by the mother even more difficult. Living with relatives is not uncommon. Some mothers will take in a boyfriend who can help financially in order to make ends meet. This situation often does not work out as planned. I have done ministry with many whose story includes four or five stepfathers or boyfriends, at least one of whom was abusive.

Gary Heese

Miscarriage or Stillbirth

TIME OF GRIEF

The loss of a child—whether accidental or by the will of the parent—requires a similar ministry application to free seekers from the burden they carry. If applicable, encourage them to allow a time for grieving over the loss of the child. This may be taking place as they are sharing with you, so allow a reasonable length of time for them to go through that. Allow them to express their anger as well. When the time is right, you may eventually inquire whether they can ask God to forgive them for the anger they have toward Him. The woman who has lost a child may grieve that loss for a long time and even continue to feel responsible for the care of that baby.

TIME TO RELEASE

As helpers, we want to coach seekers to recognize that they were not designed to carry the burden they are carrying. My discourse with them will look something like this: "I think you have carried this responsibility long enough. If you haven't released your baby to the Lord, I think it would be good to do that." The father sometimes has a similar experience. In the case of a miscarriage or a stillbirth, the men seem to have an easier time with relinquishment than the mothers.

PRAYING WITH THE MOTHER

Lead her to pray and release the baby to the Lord, you may even ask her if she would like to name the baby. In the case of a stillbirth baby, some grief ministries recommend having a memorial service and perhaps plant a tree or some other sort of remembrance for the child. In the case of a miscarriage, some sort of recognition is also meaningful.

DEAL WITH THE FATHER

Often the father does not share the same level of grief as the mother. This is not uncommon. As a result, he may not have been emotionally supportive and may even have said hurtful things to his wife because of the way she is reacting to the loss. Men just don't have the emotional connection a woman does. When this has happened, it helps to walk the couple through resolving this difference. If the father seems indifferent to the loss of an infant, the mother can be deeply offended. She may not be able to understand why he doesn't display the same level of emotion she does from the loss. Generally, men are able to process miscarriages and stillborn infants in a more rational than emotional way. The experience, for men, is simply different than it is for the mother.

Abortion

In the case of abortion, some really haven't gotten in touch with the depth of what they have done. They may not come to terms with what abortion actually is for decades. When they do acknowledge the depth of what they have done, they may be overwhelmed with guilt, shame, and possibly a flood of other emotions.

Dissociation

Some have mentally placed the baby in a compartment where the baby has not yet been identified as a living being. I have seen some women talk through their decision as though the baby was identified as a familiar medical term, which classifies the baby as something other than a living being, and the mother can remain stuck in that frame of mind for decades. I have found that when I stop and ask the mother to pray with me about the event, she quickly receives revelation of the extent of what happened and then moves immediately from understanding to repentance. When this happens, freedom begins to come.

I once ministered to a health-care worker who had decided years before to have an abortion. She had been trained in the accepted terminology of procedures in the hospital. There were different terms and ways to identify the embryo that was removed instead of giving it an identity that assumed existence or life. She was so ingrained with this vocabulary that she could easily dismiss the notion that the one she had aborted was a living being. When we prayed about the event, she broke into tears and wept for the child she had aborted. She began asking God for forgiveness.

Guilt and Shame

When seekers are aware of the sin committed, we can suggest what they need to repent of. They will often repent on their own for the sin of murder. In some cases I will suggest they renounce the spirit of murder. I have seen cases where a mother has difficulty accepting her surviving children and is disciplining them in anger. Renouncing the spirit of murder could help in this situation.

I confront this area as gently as possible and only for the purpose of helping them find freedom. If the mother was a Christian before she had the abortion, we ask if she would like to ask forgiveness from us as representatives of the body of Christ. We can also help her ask God to forgive her.

Depending on her relationship with the father of the child, we might want to ask about any offenses in that relationship. She may need to forgive the father of the baby; she might also consider breaking soul ties with the father; and she may want to pray about inappropriate authority as well.

RELEASE

As with miscarriages and stillborn children, we want to coach seekers to recognize they are carrying a burden they were not intended to carry. The discourse will look something like this: "If you haven't released your baby to the Lord, I think it would be good to do that. I think you have carried this responsibility long enough."

It is important to realize the father may have similar burdens. The father of an aborted child will sometimes carry the same level of guilt and shame the mother does. We ministered to a fifty-three-year-old man whose girlfriend had an abortion when he was seventeen. He did not want his girlfriend to abort the child; he wanted to marry her. She and her father went to an abortion clinic three hours away from their hometown and had the abortion done without the father's knowledge.

The father, thirty-six years later, was still not married and felt shame for the abortion. He still cried about his unborn child and for many years believed he deserved to be punished for getting his girlfriend pregnant. After all this time he was finally able to shed the thousand-pound pack he'd been carrying on his back.

Praying with the Mother

Lead her to pray and release the baby to the Lord. Ask her if she would like to name the baby. I sometimes suggest a ministry specifically designed for post abortion called Rachel's Vineyard. This ministry is easily found online, and local seminars occur in several states throughout the year.

Breaking Soul Ties

Relationship with the Heavenly Father

In our personal ministry time with individuals, we eventually offer the seeker an opportunity to break soul ties with previous partners with whom they have had inappropriate relationships. This can be crucial for someone to feel worthy of coming into a relationship with their heavenly Father.

I have found it to be somewhat counterproductive to do Father heart ministry with anyone before doing soul ties ministry. Many feel the need to "get cleaned up" before coming into a relationship with their heavenly Father. I highly recommend this prayer ministry for the issues of fornication, adultery, incest, rape, homosexual relations, prostitution, bestiality, and even divorce. It is optional with widows by modification of the prayer used and only if the survivor is ready to do so for the purpose of remarriage. The following are suggested steps in the procedure:

Invite the Holy Spirit

Seekers can simply ask the Lord to show them who they need to break soul ties with. Make a chronological list of each person they have had an inappropriate relationship with. Consider who they may have defiled, and who may have defiled them. In the same way, consider who might have had inappropriate authority over them during some period of their life.

Be Specific

Address each relationship or incident separately. Grouping the incidents together will shorten the ministry time but will not help the seeker. Seekers who do not know the person's name can describe the place where they met (the guy from Jake's bar). Many times, the Holy Spirit will reveal to the seeker additional people or instances that need to be dealt with as ministry proceeds.

Call the Sin What It Is

It's not "Lord, forgive me for *my wrong relationship* with Bob." Instead, it's "Lord forgive me for *the sin of adultery* with Bob …."

Seekers will come to a greater depth of release if they call the sin what it is. God is specific; He does not speak in euphemisms. In other words, to ask forgiveness for "hooking up" with someone will not bring a seeker to the same depth of repentance and healing as asking forgiveness for "committing the sin of fornication."

Possible Examples

Inappropriate touching, fantasy lust, pornography, molestation, fornication, adultery, prostitution, homosexuality, rape, incest, and bestiality are some specific sexual sins to consider repenting of specifically.

Spirits to Address

Sometimes the Holy Spirit will point out specific spirits or behaviors to renounce also. I will address these behaviors with a tentative statement like "Is it possible you had a seductive spirit?" or "Would you like to renounce the unclean spirit?" (At times an unclean spirit has been present with illicit sexual sins such as prostitution, rape, incest, bestiality, and homosexuality.) Along with any sexual assault, I ask if they would like to also renounce the inappropriate authority and the spirit of slavery. (I have watched incest survivors come to life before my eyes as they renounce the spirit of slavery and recognize they are free!)

Cleansing Prayer

Once a seeker has been led through breaking soul ties, we stop for a moment and ask the Holy Spirit to come and bring to remembrance any other events to address at this time. We then continue with a cleansing prayer, because it is just as important to pray over them for cleansing. We have had testimonies that this part of the ministry is as meaningful as anytime they have ever been prayed over. Invite the Holy Spirit to come and cleanse them from head to toe. Starting from the head, pray for cleansing over the whole person: the mind, ears, nose, mouth, torso, private parts, hands, etc.

Inappropriate Authority

Inappropriate authority occurs when a person attempts to control someone through domination, manipulation, oppression, or guilt trips. Inappropriate authority is usually not recognized by individuals until they are well into their adult years. After explaining inappropriate authority to a seeker, I will ask: "Who in your life has inappropriate authority?"

Some will answer: "Everyone!"

The common thread I have found with adults who have these kinds of relationships is the violation of authority in their childhood. Some authority figure abused or controlled them at an early age. When this happens, a spirit of slavery often takes hold of the person along with the inappropriate authority. If this is the case, relationships that follow are seldom healthy relationships. A predator can identify a person they can control or abuse out of a crowd. It is as though incest or rape victims have a sign on their backs as teens and adults that says, "I'm an easy target." These victims don't have a good opinion of themselves; they have been so devalued, dishonored, and disrespected as human beings that they don't believe they deserve something better.

Inappropriate authority is unmistakably present from involuntary sex acts. Those who have been molested, raped, or sexually abused or have been victims of incest can find freedom when delivered from the inappropriate authority in their lives.

SPIRITS TO ADDRESS

Lead the seeker to renounce spirits possibly present with inappropriate authority: The spirit of slavery, the spirit of witchcraft, the spirit of antichrist, in the case of sexual sin, an unclean spirit.

Gary Heese

Sexual Abuse, Molestation, or Incest

Move Slowly, But Keep Moving

Ministry with survivors of sexual abuse can take time and patience in order to build relationship and trust. They need, first of all, to tell their story, as all other victims do. They need to acknowledge, "This is who I am, and this is where I came from." Most of the survivors we have worked with over the years had already worked through this phase with a professional counselor. Some had been seeing counselors for years prior to getting help from the church. They could usually talk about the past with composure because of the hard work they had been through with a counselor.

I find it helpful to assure them that where they came from does not have to be who they are now. Because of what Jesus has done for them on the cross, they have been redeemed, removed from the pit and set upon "the Rock." We want to help them keep moving forward in the process of healing, so be careful not to allow them to talk about the same issues repeatedly. Encourage them to begin forgiving and to be specific about what they are forgiving for.

Knowing the culture of those who've been abused is especially helpful in this ministry model. There are many different ways a person can be violated in this area. When coaching the Seeker through forgiveness, I suggest some of the many possible offenses within this area of offense. The seeker has probably already shared some of those specific offenses if you have spent time together. Our job as the helper is to help seekers cover as many of these offenses as possible. We will be more effective if we are familiar with their culture in order to help them walk through this process.

Soul Ties First?

Many times I have had to begin with breaking soul ties and inappropriate authority in order to help the seeker gain enough composure or strength to deal with the entire offense. When I see the need for this, I make it pretty simple. I ask them if they would like to break soul ties with the abuser and I begin leading them in the soul tie prayer (found in the prayer section of chapter 4).

What to Forgive

Some of the basic offenses related to this violation are fear, dishonor, disrespect, shaming, betrayal, stealing of innocence, stealing their childhood, defilement, being devalued, rejection as a daughter and being taken as a mistress (incest), manipulation, inappropriate authority, lying about the abuse and not taking responsibility, enslavement, deception, and humiliation. The depth of wounding will vary with individuals depending on the following variables: the age at which the abuse started; the number of times and extent of the abuse; whether it was exposure, touching, or penetration; the personality of the person abused; how the offense was handled when it was discovered, if any action was taken at all—and all of this multiplied by the length of time over which the offense occurred.

Whom to Forgive

Often what hurts most is the parent who didn't protect the child from the abuse. In most cases where this applies, the mother knew what was happening but did nothing about it. In some cases, when the child informs the mother of the offense, the sin is not reported or is not acknowledged as an offense. One mother brushed off the violation as unimportant. She also had been abused by a family member as a child and told her daughter to just get over it. And in some cases when the child finally summons enough courage to tell someone, the parent accuses the child of lying or denies it ever happened. Either way, the child feels (and is) devalued. When the adult child confronts the mother in such cases, often the mother denies that she knew anything about the abuse or makes an excuse about not knowing where to go or how to provide for the child if the abuser had left. Sadly, many times the mother was aware of the abuse but did not want to cause a conflict within the family or risk losing the financial security. It is not uncommon for victims to have more resentment toward the parent who failed to protect them than toward the abuser.

The seeker may also need to forgive the other parent for being absent in some cases. In the case of divorce, perhaps the mother remarried and the abuse comes from a stepfather or a member of the stepfamily. The child may be angrier with the biological father because this never would have happened if Dad hadn't left.

Some families have feared confronting the uncle who was abusing their children because embarrassment might come to the family. The welfare of the children is not a primary concern. Another concern is how the family would be torn apart by truth coming out.

What to Do with Shame

The victim struggles with false guilt and shame simply because of the illicit act that incest is. The social norm is one cause of shame with incest survivors. The abuser will sometimes manipulate the child, twisting the truth by making the child believe it was something the child had done which attracted the abuser; the child fixed her hair really cute that day or put on a dress that tempted the abuser.

The cruelest trap is when the predator gives gifts or money after an incident. Children who accept a gift from the abuser may feel deserving at the time. Later on, however, the child usually feels guilty and eventually equates accepting the gift with prostitution. The result: now the child has another cause for shame.

Another common cause for shame is that children feel guilty because they didn't tell someone sooner. It is also possible for them to struggle with guilt because within the act of abuse, some part of it felt good, which may have inhibited them from telling someone about it sooner. In some cases, the child even experiences an orgasm. This response to stimulation is natural, but many will feel guilty or sick to have responded to such a foul act committed against them. To lead the seeker to freedom, each cause of shame may need to be addressed.

How to Pray

If the seeker accepted a gift, help them understand that they were manipulated. Leading them through the prayer to break inappropriate authority and soul ties is a given. In order to free seekers of the guilt for accepting a gift, ask if they would like to ask God to forgive them for prostitution. Then ask them if they can forgive themselves. If applicable, ask if they want to ask forgiveness for not telling someone about it sooner. Then, again, ask them to forgive themselves.

A Light Came On

We have ministered to several incest survivors over the years. Many times, during the soul tie ministry, we have asked them to pray and renounce the inappropriate authority and the spirit of slavery. These seekers were under the control of their abusers even though they might not have seen the perpetrators for decades. Some were even being controlled from the grave. They will raise their head following that prayer, open their eyes and you can see it is like for them they have been in darkness and the lights were turned on. Hallelujah!

Because God made us to be sexual beings, we can ask God to cleanse them of the perversion they have experienced and also ask God to restore them. Finally, ask the Holy Spirit to cleanse them from all defilement. Cleanse them from head to toe by calling on the blood of Jesus to cleanse every part of them, including their private parts.

The cleansing prayer can be as significant as breaking soul ties can be. When seekers have finished breaking soul ties, you can pray a cleansing prayer over them. We ask the Holy Spirit to cleanse a seeker from all unrighteousness by His power and the blood of Jesus. Then we ask for the cleansing of the entire being, taking time to pray separately for each one—from mind, eyes, nose, mouth, and torso to private parts. In the breaking of other soul ties, we also pray for the Holy Spirit to cleanse their feet, which have taken them places to commit inappropriate sexual acts outside the covenant of marriage. We declare that "by the power of the Holy Spirit and the cleansing blood of Jesus (seekers name)_____is clean."

In cases of sexual immorality, inappropriate authority, and abuse, there are times we suggest the Seeker go home and take a bath or shower, asking the Holy Spirit to cleanse them and let the defilement of the past go down the drain.

Following a ministry time of this nature, I recommend the helper also go home and pray with a friend or spouse to cleanse yourself of any defilement you have received from the confessions you've just heard.

Domestic Violence

A History of Abuse

I have seen an obvious correlation between women who were abused as children and those who are in abusive relationships as adults. I have seen many women stuck in violent relationships who are not trying to leave those relationships. Nearly all had a history of at least physical and emotional abuse as a child, and most had been sexually abused or molested as children also. From their life experiences, they have developed a sense of low self-worth, often feeling as if they don't deserve anything better. After listening to so many of their stories, I saw that because of their history, they didn't have the ability or emotional strength to leave the relationship and make healthy choices for themselves. Some of them are incapable of saying the word *no* to someone who appears to be in any position of authority over them.

Begin Referring Early

When suspecting an abuser is the problem, refer the women to the local ministry specifically designed to help them with "safe house" support groups, professional counselors for themselves and any children they have, and legal assistance. We can continue offering assistance through the process by praying for them and being there for them as well. We can demonstrate caring by giving a phone number they can call in times of need.

SOME FEAR FOR THEIR LIVES

Men who seduce women into a relationship and then begin with the abuse are adept at what they do. It's almost as if they've attended seminars on manipulation, oppression, and control, and they use these evil skills cleverly to abuse others. Upon the outset of the relationship, one will present himself as a prince riding a white stallion. The women on whom these men have artfully set their sights feel so fortunate to have found their prince that they readily believe their lies.

While red flags would be popping up in full view for the rest of us, these victims are unable to see the warning signs. The abuser's charm enables him to quickly go from first base to a home run in the relationship. This draws the woman into a soul tie and hope for a bright future. Such a man is skilled at making the woman feel dependent on him. He has ways of separating her emotionally and physically from any support system, friends, family, and church. If she becomes pregnant, she feels even more dependent upon him.

One of the warning signs is obsessive calling, texting, or e-mailing. He might come by her job frequently to check up on her. He may even manipulate her to the point that she loses her job. Now she is even more dependent on him. (One variation of this scenario is that she has a very good job and the man quits his job, if he had one. Now he can stay at home and drink beer or do drugs she has paid for.) He will begin to be critical and judgmental, tearing her down emotionally. He will become envious or jealous of any other relationship she has. He will begin to check phone calls, Facebook, and e-mails, questioning everything until the woman is afraid to have a normal communication or friendship with anyone. He will find fault in every friend and relative she has. The woman becomes isolated and fearful of reaching out to anyone. She will be the one who ends up apologizing for everything.

The physical abuse may not begin for several months or until after the baby is born. The abuse will increase in intensity as the relationship goes on. The more control he has gained, the more severe the abuse will become. The power and control increases in stages: they begin by dating; then somehow they are living together; then she is pregnant; he begins to have control over her income; now they are married; now she finds herself separated from her friends and family; and somehow, in the end, she is completely dependent upon him. The woman has begun to doubt her own judgment, and she no longer has a clear definition of right and wrong. Because of the demonic force the woman is under, she has a difficult time making decisions and making healthy choices. I am convinced these men are ruling with a demonic force.

THERE IS GOOD IN HIM

I hear this from every woman at some point during the interview: "He has a lot of good in him. I love him." And so she stays, believing that if she can behave and not make him angry, he will change, and eventually things will get better. *Not!* I have had about a 1 percent success rate in getting an abuser to change. Why? Because he doesn't have a problem. Some have agreed to counseling for maybe one visit, to get the woman back if they are separated. As soon as he has regained control, he ends the charade and resumes the abuse.

Fear of the children being hurt can be the deal breaker in the relationship. Most women will seek help if it seems that the children are in danger.

Break Inappropriate Authorities of the Past

I have helped many to break free from these types of relationships. The first thing I suggest is leading them in the prayer to break inappropriate authority. It is very possible this man is not the first inappropriate authority in a seeker's life. I ask her to consider who else in her life was abusive, dominating, manipulative, or controlling. Then I lead her through the prayer to break soul ties and inappropriate authorities from past and present relationships (one at a time). I also lead her to break soul ties with the present abuser and renounce the spirit of slavery, and even a spirit of antichrist. This will sometimes provoke a manifestation of some kind when deliverance comes.

Forgiveness is still necessary. Forgiveness needs to happen first for any deliverance or change to occur. That doesn't mean any woman needs to continue in an abusive relationship.

A support group is helpful for them to begin making healthy choices. Most churches and communities have social services to help women in need. Safe havens, counseling, legal advice, and other forms of assistance are available. The key is getting the woman away from her environment long enough to help her. The support group is vital for helping her become aware of other options and for giving hope. The group can also help her achieve the renewing of her mind and see her value as a person. We can lead her through prayer for all the hurts, rejections, and regrets in her life. When she begins to experience the power of the cross in her life, it will give her strength as well.

Unwed or Single Mothers

Unwed mothers are among the bravest lot I have had the privilege to know. It is not uncommon to find they haven't received any financial support from the father. Sadly, it is common for men to abandon the mother and child, choosing to have nothing or little to do with them. When the mother sees the result in her child of being raised in a single parent home, she often blames herself that the father is not involved in her child's life. Add on to this the shame and regret from being an unwed mother to the already unlimited responsibility of the single mom, and you have a person on overload.

I have worked with a number of young women who have gotten pregnant with a man they never intended to marry. In fact, some have even aborted the pregnancy to avoid raising a child with a man they thought was great for a season but later learned was not who he appeared to be. They couldn't fathom ever trusting the man with the care of their child, so having the baby didn't seem like a viable option. I am not saying they made the correct choice. Their choice was made out of fear and not knowing how to ensure the child would have a good life.

They Need Help

I believe single mothers are under more stress and responsibility than any other life position. When left with sole responsibility to provide for a child's needs, many will jump into a relationship, hoping to find emotional and financial support. I frequently hear from single mothers that they feel overwhelmed. Some are holding down a part-time job, going to school, and being a mom while trying to pay the bills and put food on the table.

Children in single-parent homes often display behavioral problems down the road, simply because they do not have a strong male authority nearby the way God intended. The children, of course, do not know why they are acting out or why they are so angry. They suffer from a love deficit, and they are doing the only thing they know to fill it. They don't know the source of their pain; they are simply trying to make the pain go away.

MINISTERING TO GUILT AND SHAME

Guilt and shame are already present from being an unwed mother. If the woman was raised in a Christian home, that shame will be magnified by the commandment that has been tested: "Honor your father and mother, and things will go well with you" (see Exodus 20:12). The consequence is obvious: when we dishonor our father and mother, things will not go so well. So the unwed mother will carry the burden of guilt and shame indefinitely if she has no understanding of how to cast it off. Every mother says the same thing: "Don't get me wrong. I love my child, and he or she means the world to me." Our goal as a helper is to relieve some of the emotional stress these mothers are carrying by leading them through times of prayer to free them from guilt and shame. Because of the guilt most mothers ignore a child's behavior and refrain from proper discipline.

The following are a few of the common bondages to address in this ministry model:

Forgiveness for dishonor. In many families, having a child before marriage would be dishonor to the family. This would be more obvious in a Christian home. It is a great to ask God to forgive.

Ask the body of Christ to forgive. Those raised in a Christian home have also sinned against the body of Christ. As a helper you can stand in as a representative of the body of Christ and have the mother ask you to forgive her.

Forgive themselves. They could also forgive themselves for the sin of fornication, choosing the father they chose for their child, dishonoring their family, dishonoring themselves, making poor choices (whatever those choices may have been), and for being irresponsible.

Forgive the father. Forgive the father for his irresponsibility, abandonment, rejection, lack of financial support, and substance abuse if applicable. Other specifics will become clear from listening to the story.

Break soul ties. I would also recommend breaking soul ties with the father or ex-husband and possibly break inappropriate authority.

Renounce the shame and guilt.

Relinquish. Many of these mothers believe it is their responsibility to be both mother and father to their child. Help them understand that God is the child's father. These mothers often expect themselves to be something they can't possibly be. Help them pray and release that responsibility to God. Encourage them to coach the child into a relationship with the heavenly Father.

Pray a blessing over the mother, commending her for choosing life for her child and asking Jesus to take her shame and cleanse her from all unrighteousness.

Next step. If the mother's parents are alive, encourage her to go to them and ask their forgiveness for the dishonor she brought them. This is often a good next step. Of course, in some family situations, this procedure will not be possible. In that case, having her ask God for forgiveness, and forgiving herself, is sufficient.

Divorced single moms. Many of the above steps would apply for the divorced single mother as well. A few others might also apply. She may want to ask God forgiveness for divorce. Some might ask God forgiveness for their part in the divorce or for not trying to work out the conflict. They may even ask the children to forgive them, as well as their ex-husbands. And finally they also could forgive themselves.

Addictions

THE FIRST ATTEMPT

A rehab facility or twelve-step program may be one of the first resources an addict uses to begin the recovery or healing process. The twelve steps are a good next step after rehab. Sooner or later, the addict needs to work through the spiritual bondages as well.

Many addicts are driven to their addiction initially because of pain in their lives. We learned in counseling school that when we have an emotional pain from our past, our human response is to swing to a pleasure. When we swing to the pleasure frequently, eventually the pleasure becomes destructive and has control over us. Then we lose control of our lives. The loving parent or spouse often believes the best way to help is by taking control for the addict. The parent or spouse eventually begins taking responsibility for the addict's behavior. The best course of action, however, instead of taking responsibility for the addict's behavior, is to help them want to get better by releasing them to the Lord.

DENIAL

Twelve-step programs are great for bringing the addict out of denial, providing a place of ongoing support, accountability, and changing old habits and lifestyles. Acknowledging and accepting who I am and where I came from is the beginning of healing. Similar to a basic counseling process, a twelve-step program may help seekers identify their pain, but the application of healing is limited in these programs. When working with someone who is beginning this process for the first time, realize that addicts commonly attempt rehab in a facility three to five times before they really decide they want to change.

REGRETS

Addicts in recovery are often drawn back into their addiction because of their regrets. They stop using long enough to reflect on what they've done and everyone they have hurt and disappointed, and they feel such hatred for themselves that they attempt to kill this new pain with further substance abuse. Some eventually begin making better choices after their doctor has told them they will die if they don't quit. But since many are trying to destroy themselves anyway, bad news from the doctor doesn't always make a difference. Very effective elements of twelve-step groups are accountability and the sponsor who is there to help addicts with encouragement in their weak moments. The sponsors who are former addicts themselves—have walked the path before and know when an addict is lying or manipulating and can effectively confront the one in recovery.

Christian Twelve Step

We have had Christian twelve-step groups in our church for many years. The advantage of these groups is their integration of biblical principles and the use of Scripture. There is also basic discipleship in the Christian recovery groups. This also provides addicts with a great place to make new friends, which combats the pitfall of falling back into the same environment and circle of friends they came out of.

The members of these Christian twelve-step groups pray for each other and emphasize dependence on Jesus Christ to make a difference, which is helpful, but this does not equal some of the needs that are met by your local AA groups. The program in a church typically meets once a week, whereas AA is always open. Some addicts, in the beginning of recovery, are at the AA meeting hall three to five times a day. Depending on where a person is in recovery, this may meet a specific need.

Celebrate Recovery is the recovery group in the church to which I refer addicts. CR is a wonderful gate of entry for a person needing to get into church life. A number of changes are imperative in order for an addict to succeed in recovery. The church offers a number of options to help make those changes. There might be a need to change jobs or place of residence, to gain a new circle of friends, or make any number of other changes. One way to succeed in making better choices is to remove the option for bad choices. Eventually, we encourage those in CR to do a spiritual inventory to pray through the bondages with a helper. In this process, they are encouraged and taught how to pray through hurts and regrets of their past. The level of healing the Holy Spirit is willing to do simply can't be matched by any man-made program.

Relinquish

Dragging someone we love to one of these programs will not help. The most effective and successful way of getting addicts to seek help is through relinquishment. Release them to the Lord, and allow them to experience the consequences of their behavior. They may lose their family, job, house, car, and driver's license. They might end up homeless or incarcerated. God may need to use drastic measures in order to get an addict's attention. The more you try to help by protecting or rescuing, the more you will enable the acting out. This will only result in a further descent into addiction.

After watching this pattern in several different families, I could see one common factor. Each parent or spouse stuck in this pattern struggled with unbelief. Each one is and has been a controlling parent or spouse, still trying to control the addict's behavior or take responsibility for the one in need. They do not trust that God is in control. The parent or spouse is attempting to be the person's savior.

Some young people are even driven to their addiction by a controlling parent. In such cases, the kids are looking for something they can control, whether it's an eating disorder, inappropriate sexual behavior, drugs, or alcohol. Others resort to an addiction to kill the pain from their past and are then kept within the grip of the addiction by the controlling parent.

We tie God's hands when we take control, because He will always respect our free will. Many of us want to be the savior, but there is only one Savior, and you are not Him. If you are guilty of trying to control others (even if your intentions are good), try repenting, asking God to forgive you, and release your family member to the Lord.

Many Bondages

When ministering to addicts who finally want help, we may find that numerous bondages need to be addressed. What is the pain they are trying so desperately to escape? Addictions are often a generational sin. The addiction might even skip a generation, but the effect of the curse is still there. This doesn't give the addict an excuse, but it is true that descendants of an addict have a propensity toward addictive behavior. These addictive behaviors could be excessive exercising, workaholism, an eating disorder, or any of several other compulsive behaviors.

Any substance abuse is an act of idolatry. Addicts are turning to drugs or alcohol rather than God for their needs. According to Scripture, the use of drugs is an act of sorcery. You can ask them to renounce the sorcery. What are the regrets to be addressed, the "I should have's or "I shouldn't have's of their past? They can ask God for forgiveness, and they need to forgive themselves. And of course, the next step in recovery is going to those they have hurt, stolen from, offended, or shamed and asking forgiveness.

Identificational Repentance

In Touch with the Pain

This ministry is used sometimes in the event a seeker is not getting in touch with the feelings of a hurt. A significant element of the healing comes from visiting the event, with all its pain, and inviting God in to bring healing and speak truth into the difficult time. In such cases, the helper can stand in the gap between a seeker and a parent who is not present and ask forgiveness. The helper can say something like "I know I'm not your father, but as a father who also has not been good to their kids, would you forgive me?"

This can also apply for leaders. During one class, a young woman shared that she had been going to a pastor for counseling. The two ended up having an affair. In the same ministry group was a pastor who had fallen into an affair with one of his church members. We had the two come together, and he asked her to forgive him for taking advantage of his authority as a leader. In this model, both received healing.

Forgiveness of Previous Generations

This ministry is significant when discrimination or the advantage of authority is used against someone and is part of their wounding. I have stood in the gap as a representative of the white oppressors in this situation. I have asked the seeker to forgive me as the representative of the injustice, abuse, and violation of human rights by our ancestors.

I have also used this ministry with individuals from different nations who carry resentment for one another because of the wars their nations have fought during previous generations.

Caution

When standing in as a father or mother, it is possible to form a bond that causes the seeker to be dependent on you. We cannot be someone's mother or father. Only God can do that. God may use us occasionally to minister His Father's heart (or mother heart) toward someone, but if we try to take the place of their mother or father, eventually we will fail. We will not be able to be what they need or be there when they need us. When this happens—and it will—only more wounding will occur. Our goal in this ministry is always to point them to Jesus and their heavenly Father for what they are lacking.

Performance Orientation

Some seekers are very competitive and tend to be overachievers. They also commonly suffer from perfectionism. It is a common condition among Christians and in society as a whole. The people believe they must somehow *earn* or *deserve* any gift from God. Their minds and spirits are aware of the free gift of salvation, but the heart may retain the habit of earning love by performing; strife, tension, fear, and incorrect motives impel this person. There is nothing wrong with performing and working hard, but performance-oriented people find themselves driven to work hard for reasons that are inappropriate in God's kingdom.

The underlying sins (and it's difficult to understand that this *is* sin) of performance orientation are fear of people, fear of failure, self-righteousness (sin of the Pharisees, a religious spirit), hidden resentment, defensiveness, anger, denial, anxiety, condemnation, guilt, criticism, superiority, and bondage to others. The root cause is *unbelief.*

Perfectionism is spiritual distortion, a counterfeit of Christian perfection. It is the "tyranny of the oughts" like bondage, depression, etc. Both performance orientation and perfectionism are a form of legalism.

Galatians 3:1 asks "Who has bewitched you?" In the Living Bible, "What magician has hypnotized you and cast an evil spell upon you?"

It's necessary to renounce the curse and gain a proper understanding of *grace*. Grace means "freely given, undeserved, unmerited, unearnable, and unrepayable favor." Our Father's loving acceptance of us has nothing to do with our worthiness. He accepts us because of what Christ has done for us—and He is the One who sent Christ to do it!

THE CAUSES

- Deep-rooted rejection, usually from an early age.
- Feeling of inadequacy and inferiority.
- Hidden resentment from the past, especially early childhood.
- Lack of proper identity and security in Christ.
- Bitter root judgment and expectancy are often present.
- Sibling rivalry.
- Parents have instilled a competitive spirit in the child by tying acceptance to their performance.
- Shame based: they were never good enough because of criticism and judgment.
- A distorted view of what "success" is.

OFTEN A MAJOR CRISIS OCCURS

A crisis can arise such as a nervous breakdown, alcoholism, gambling, adultery, divorce, high blood pressure, or another sickness. Living in an environment where lack of acceptance prevails or a lack of affirmation can drive someone into the performance trap.

THE TREATMENT

1. Identify the root cause of the behavior. Apply redemption where needed.
2. Bring the problem clearly into view. It is not a small flaw, but is rather a serious cancer, affecting the entire personality.
3. The person must come to hate it and turn from it in repentance.
4. Prayer for the person by a *trained helper* can make a big difference by reaching the inner-child with love and forgiveness.
5. The seeker can verbally renounce the whole pattern of performance.

PRACTICING THE PRESENCE OF GOD

The abiding presence of Christ helps overcome performance orientation. It provides a deep sense of acceptance and affirmation from the Father, helping us secure our proper identity. It is wonderfully healing and promotes a state of rest to the soul. Hebrews 4:11 says, "Let us therefore be diligent to enter that rest, lest anyone fall according to the same example of disobedience." It is the secret of sanctification.

Suicide

Suicide is another option many try before seeking God's help. I have ministered to many who had difficult life events they could not handle and had attempted or considered suicide as an option for relief or escape. Many of the previously mentioned challenges or bondages some face can cause them to make such choices. Their belief system may be so challenged with lies they believed that they eventually conclude that "I have no value," "I don't matter," "I am worthless," or another falsehood from a very long list.

When I have ministered to those who have attempted or considered suicide, I have identified the bondages they struggle with and offered to walk them through those they relate to. Eventually they begin to see hope. I think *hope* is a great cure for suicide. With nearly every seeker who struggles with thoughts of suicide, one of the significant bondages identified is curses.

As I have shared in several stories, a curse of death is a common deduction for many. At some point in the process of renouncing the curses of death, I lead them to Deuteronomy 30:19, where God's Word says, "I call heaven and earth as witnesses today against you, that I have set before you life and death, blessing and cursing; therefore choose life, that both you and your descendants may live …." I offer seekers this choice. I ask them to repent of the thought or attempt of suicide I then lead them to pray and declare, "Today I choose life". I have never had anyone decline this choice.

Father/Mother Heart Ministry

THE PARENT'S ROLE

This is not breaking news: parents are proven to have the strongest influence in an individual's life. Therefore, this ministry can be very powerful in bringing healing to the father and mother wounds. God designed the family with the responsibility of the father being to provide security, value, and identity to his children. The mother's responsibility is to provide compassion, mercy, and nurturing. If any of these needs are unmet, children will go to other places searching for someone or something to fill the need or complete them. The more needs are unmet in the family, the broader the love deficit within the child grows. It is as though the child has a hole in her or his heart.

Our goal in this ministry is to provide understanding and a safe place for seekers to receive a greater revelation of who God is as their Father. Our place as a child of God is, in itself, our "identity in Christ." Only God can fill the void or hole in a seeker's heart.

This ministry is most effective after seekers have prayed through the hurts of their past and have forgiven offenses, relinquished and broken soul ties, and been through the cleansing from sexual sins and violations. It is a known reality that unforgiveness separates us from God. Paul tells us to "run from sexual sin," because "all other sins are committed outside the body." That's what God says, so it must be true. Because of this, sexual sin has the ability to make a person feel so unworthy and even unclean that they cannot come into the presence of their heavenly Father because of the shame they feel.

The following is a worksheet I often use, especially in group ministry, to lead others into that place to receive God as their Father.

Father Heart of God Worksheet

1. Pray and forgive those you have not completely forgiven. Consider the specific events and the related offenses to those events.
2. Give up the right to the "if only"s. Relinquish your rights to God.
3. Pray and repent of vows you may have made about an authority figure, and renounce them.
4. Ask forgiveness for the judgments of an authority figure in your life.

5. Ask God forgiveness for any way you dishonored your parents.
6. Ask forgiveness for any offense to the body of Christ.
7. Ask God forgiveness for comparing Him to your earthly authority figures.
8. Choose to believe what God's Word says about Him.
9. What new <u>attributes</u> would you like to have in your belief system about who God is?
10. Acknowledge your need for Him. Then pray and receive Him as your Father.

How to Offer Father Heart Ministry

After completing and reviewing the ministry principles, which include forgiving; relinquishing their rights; and breaking vows, curses, judgments, and soul ties, it's time to pray. Pray for God to come and bring healing to the seeker's heart, fill the void, and reveal his or her true value and dearness. We pray for God to restore seekers' identity and where they have been rejected, to know His acceptance. This is a great time to read Scripture that is applicable. One suggestion is Psalm 139.

Restore the Soul

For some, such as incest survivors, we ask God to restore their soul (the mind, will, and emotions). The purpose of this is to bring in the opposite spirit from that of their life experience. While doing this, you may be embracing them in something like a "bear hug." Carla and I will often embrace a seeker together as a couple. The Spirit may lead you to actually set them on your lap. The truth is that someone in pain often needs the love of God to flow through the physical touch of a believer. The Bible says for the elders to "lay hands on" people in certain instances. Some will not receive the depth of healing otherwise. God can heal some of the deepest hurts, at the same time filling the void with His love. The use of physical touch is the most significant advantage of lay counseling and pastoral ministry.

Getting in Touch

We ministered once to a young lady I will call Maria. Carla and I were working in a counseling school in our mission. When Maria first came to our room, she wanted to see family photos. She was curious and asked many questions about what we did with our kids and how we functioned as a family. We shared with her some of the memorable times we had as a family and the many fun things we did together. Maria shared with us the difficult times she remembered from her family life and how most of her childhood was spent taking care of her mother and other siblings. Maria's mother suffered from manic depression and spent most of her time in bed. As a result, Maria never received affirmation or affection as a child.

Maria was angry with God for the parents she had and the childhood she lost. After several ministry sessions, we were able to do some significant Father/mother heart ministry with her. It changed her life to finally feel as if she had value and was lovable. She came into her true identity, and she really did bloom! Watching her over the next few weeks was like seeing someone who had been given a "makeover." Her countenance changed dramatically as she ministered to others. Her depression and shame were gone.

We have since ministered God's Father/mother heart to dozens of adult men and women. The Father Heart ministry has been life-changing for many. The fruit of this ministry is evident; as many of these seekers have gone on to serve the Lord in full-time ministry or long-term missions work.

Ministry Preparation

For the helper,

I have mentioned before my default for ministry is encouraging anyone asking for help to start with doing a spiritual inventory of their lives.

I strongly encourage the seeker I am working with to read the personal ministry booklet "Handbook to Healing". Ask them to take note of issues revealed to them from the various bondages in the booklet fill out the "Ministry Work Sheet". I know this attempt by the seeker will not be all inclusive but it will give you a place to get started. Some seekers will read half of the booklet and not fill out any items on the "Worksheet" It is not ideal but your challenge now is to help them get started telling their story anyway. You might use the Work Sheet to keep on track if needed.

It is possible that an article doesn't seem to apply them. That is OK. Some of the articles may contain a large part of their life and take some time to process. Feel free to deal with each article one at a time. For example, if you discover there are many events in the area of "Forgiveness" to address, you may have a separate ministry time for that alone and continue with the rest at another time. I have ministered to some seekers in one two hour session. Others I have done as many as forty hours of ministry with many two hour sessions.

Review the list of "Helpful Dos" and the list of "Prayer Models" before a ministry time.

May the Lord fill you with His grace and the power of the Holy Spirit as you begin this process.

Ministry Worksheet

Pray and ask God to show you:

1. Who in your past hurt you (consider authority figures)? Whom do you need to forgive and for what? List traumatic experiences for which you would like prayer.

2. What "if only"s are you holding on to and need to relinquish?

3. Describe any negative or hurtful words that may have been spoken over you—or any that you have said to yourself—whose power in your life you wish to break?

4. List any vows or judgments you want to confess and break.

5. List any generational or hereditary sins you would like to break.

6. List those with whom you might have soul ties or who have inappropriate authority in your life which you would like to break.

7. In what ways have you dishonored yourself, your parents, others, or the body of Christ?

8. List the regrets in your life. What you should have done (should haves) or things you shouldn't have done (should nots).

9. List false religions or occult involvement you want to renounce.

Prayer Models

REDEMPTIVE PRAYER MODELS

Read through the following redemptive prayers as many times as you need in order to understand the principles to apply, and then you can either follow the script or pray them in your own words. Often, the exact way some prayers are written may not apply to a certain situation. The prayer may need to be rephrased to fit the need of a particular individual. Once you know the principles behind each prayer, you can easily make adjustments as you go.

Keep in mind these prayers are not intended for the seeker to read.

They are to be used only by the helper if needed to lead the seeker.

Before ministry time, please read through these prayers on your own.

Learn the principle for each one so you will be able to apply it effectively.

Lead the seeker phrase-by-phrase (read from the sheet yourself if you need to).

Feel free to revise or adjust a prayer as needed to fit the situation.

When you are comfortable praying without these examples, please do so.

Unconfessed sins: Lord, I ask you to forgive me for the sin of _____. I ask Your forgiveness, and I repent of this sin in the name of Jesus. I pray for Your grace to walk in Your ways and be Your disciple.

Forgiving others: Lord, today I choose to forgive _____ for _____. I forgive them, and they owe me nothing.

Relinquishment of rights: I give up the right to my (dreams, expectations, needs being met, etc.) _____. God, give me a healthy perspective. I relinquish the past so I can be content in the present.

Relinquishing a person: Heavenly Father, I choose to release control of/responsibility for (name of person), and I release them into Your hands, Lord. *(I give up the right to this relationship.)*.

I choose to release (name of person) into Your hands. I release them into Your care. You are their protector, Savior, healer, and Lord.

Breaking vows: Lord, I ask You to forgive me for making this vow _____. I renounce this inner vow in the name of Jesus. It no longer has a part of me.

Bitter root judgments: God, forgive me for this bitter root judgment about _____. Lord, forgive me for making the vow (example: "I will never be like them, I will never marry someone like them," etc.). I renounce this vow in the name of Jesus, and I pray that You break any judgments I have brought upon myself.

Breaking curses spoken by another: I choose to forgive (the person's name) for saying/calling me _____. I ask You, Lord, to forgive me for believing this lie, and I renounce this curse in the name of Jesus. I break the power it has over me, and from this day forward, I choose to believe what *Your Word* says about me.

Breaking self-directed curses: God, forgive me for my unbelief and my believing the lie (negative statement or belief) I have told myself. I renounce this curse _____ in the name of Jesus. This no longer has power over me. I now choose to believe what the *Word of God* says about me.

Renouncing false religions: Lord, I confess that I have participated in/been involved in/practiced _____. I ask for Your forgiveness, and I renounce _____ in the name of Jesus.

Renouncing generational sins: Lord, I pray that You forgive me and my ancestors for the generational sin of _____. I renounce this generational sin in the name of Jesus. It cannot be passed on. I pray for Your grace to adhere to Your ways and refrain from passing this behavior on to my children.

Repentance of substance abuse: Lord, I ask that You forgive me for the use of drugs/alcohol. I ask Your forgiveness for the sorcery and the idolatry. I repent of this addiction and pray for Your grace to break it from my life. I renounce it in the name of Jesus. I choose to come to You to fulfill my needs.

Release from regrets: Lord, I ask that You forgive me for (list regrets) _____, and I forgive myself. I renounce this condemnation in the name of Jesus, and I take back any ground I gave the devil through this condemnation.

Soul tie prayer (sins seeker has committed): This prayer is used to break spirit and soul ties related to sins of inappropriate touching, adultery, fornication, homosexuality, pornography, prostitution, or bestiality. This can also be used to free one from a defilement.

Heavenly Father, I ask you to forgive me for committing the sin of (name the specific sin) with (name the person), and I take back any ground I gave the devil through this relationship. I bind, cast off, and put away from me any evil influence of their spirit over my spirit or my spirit over their spirit. I cut off any spirit and soul ties. I renounce this relationship once and for all, in the name of Jesus.

Soul tie prayer (sins committed against the seeker has): This prayer is used to break spirit and soul ties related to sins of inappropriate touching, molestation, rape, incest, defilement.

Heavenly Father, I choose to forgive (name the person), for committing the sin of (name the specific sin) against me, I take back any ground that was given the devil through this act. I bind, cast off, and put away from me any evil influence of their spirit over my spirit or my spirit. I cut off any spirit and soul ties. I renounce the unclean spirit and the spirit of slavery and I renounce this relationship once and for all, in the name of Jesus.

Inappropriate authority prayer (sins committed against seeker): This prayer may be used to break the power of an inappropriate authority in your life. Someone who was dominating, controlling, oppressive, or manipulative in a relationship. This also applies to rape and incest.

Heavenly Father, I forgive (name the person) for the inappropriate authority they had in my life (name the specific offenses), and I forgive myself for allowing it. (if applicable) I take back any ground that was given the devil through this relationship. I bind, cast off, and put away from me any evil influence of (the person's) spirit over my spirit. I cut off any spirit and soul ties. I renounce this inappropriate authority and I renounce the spirit of slavery, in the name of Jesus. They no longer have a part with me.

Note: the phrase "I forgive myself for allowing it" would not apply for any abuse during childhood.

CHAPTER 6

Rebuilding, Part I

FIVE IMPORTANT STEPS ON THE ROAD TO RECOVERY

It is crucial to understand the origin of faulty beliefs and to begin correcting them so the self-perpetuating destructive effects of those beliefs do not continue. If whatever you have been thinking about yourself has been distorted by abuse, determine not to agree with those thoughts or statements. God's message is "You're not worthless; you are special!" And He wants you to develop the skill of standing up and saying that for yourself. The five steps are

1. Identify the false beliefs that are blocking your path.
2. Look for the roots of these false beliefs and the underlying factors that are causing you to maintain them.
3. Recognize and accept these false beliefs as lies; then totally and finally renounce them.
4. Pray to God that He will wither away your false beliefs and reaffirm to you His truth concerning you.
5. Use God's Word, the Bible, to set you free from the deception of all the destructive falsehoods that have been holding you in their grip. Learn to take a stand, even argue against yourself,

in order to develop a true belief system that is not rooted and grounded in abuse. Learn not to be so harsh and critical of yourself but rather to love and accept yourself.

Renewing Your Mind

A large part of individual healing and progress in healing comes after the ministry sessions. During ministry, the seeker has experienced a certain amount of deliverance, as well as emotional healing, combined with spiritual healing. To maintain this progress, there is work one must do in order to stand firm in this new place of wholeness. We call this time the rebuilding period.

What I share with you now is one tool essential for rebuilding and is used by many to resolve conflict in relationships. This tool is designed to help seekers renew their mind and resolve conflict between them, God, and others. We use a chart we call the LERC. This chart, which examines an individual's belief system, was originally developed by another ministry, and detailed instruction of how to use this tool can be found in the book *Rational Christian Thinking* by Gary Sweeten. LERC is an acronym for *Life Event Revelation Chart*.

God uses our conflicts in life only to help us come to an understanding that something is wrong under the hood. I have been using this tool during one-on-one ministry with either individuals or couples for twenty years. I have seen revelation come to those in conflict that brings certain relief for those who use it. People who've spent years in counseling, without experiencing any lasting relief, have found the truth in one session of less than two hours. I like what Gary Smalley says in his book *DNA of Relationships*: "Life is all about relationships. Everything else is just details." Most conflicts in life are rooted in relationship. The conflict is a result of the relationship with oneself, with others, or with God.

Let's begin by looking at what causes conflict. A certain event happens which is a common *trigger* for you and causes uncomfortable feelings. These feelings either cause you to react with behavior you really don't want, or cause you to believe things that are very negative or just not true. Bottom line: this scenario often results in unwanted behavior. These *trigger* events are very similar in nature and cause us to have the same emotional response and display the same behavior time and time again. It seems as though God takes us around the same tree over and over until we finally either seek help or find a way of escape.

In order to begin breaking down the emotion that has taken place, we need to look at our belief system. What do we believe about the event that just took place? The entirety of this process I am describing is a *total emotion*. Emotion is more than merely a feeling. An emotion is made up of four parts: (1) an event, (2) a reaction, (3) a feeling, and (4) a belief. The following is a description of each part of an emotion.

(1) Event (What Happened?)

This is something that causes you to have an emotional response. It can be an outward influence, such as something someone does or says that affects you; or it can be something internal, that you may create yourself from a memory, a passing thought, or a perception. Sometimes an event causes feelings that affect you in a negative way and may cause you to do something you regret later, or it simply causes uncomfortable feelings, possibly even physical discomfort.

I have worked with some who have had thoughts and perceptions cause extreme anxiety or fear, to the point they are immobilized and often seek a physician for medication. Of course, a wide variety of unwanted feelings and behaviors may be triggered by events. Often these reactions are brought on from a childhood event which may need to be revisited in order to experience healing of that particular wound. In order to know if the LERC should be done for a particular event, we need to determine if the behavior is out of proportion with the activating event.

(2) Behavior (What Did I Do?)

Your behavior is what you decide to do when a particular event takes place. This behavior could be good or not so good. In this exercise, we are not concerned with what causes good behavior (unless someone else's tragedy brings you joy; in that case, you might consider practicing this tool). Again, we are concerned with occasions when the behavior is out of proportion with what happened during the event.

When embroiled in this behavior, it may seem like you have lost the ability to choose how you will react. The reaction is so automatic that it seems like second nature to you. It is not uncommon for someone in this situation to immediately place blame somewhere other than themselves. And of course, some will believe their reaction was justified, so there was nothing wrong with how they reacted. Example: "You made me angry" or "I have a right to be angry."

The reality, however, is that you decided to be angry. This is the part of this teaching I *did not like*. I learned from this teaching that my feelings are mine because my feelings are a product of *my* belief system. This means I am also responsible for my own behavior.

Ugh! I can no longer blame my wife or my kids for the jerk I can be sometimes.

(3) Feelings (How Did I Feel?)

Feelings are a God-given element within us that can be good sometimes and not so good other times. Feelings can dictate whether we are kind or rude, angry or sad, and whether we engage in a relationship or withdraw. Some people have a difficult time describing how they feel about something. They can only express what they think. If this is true for you, you might try using a table of feelings to help you establish a vocabulary for emotions. Conversely, you may be one with an acute awareness of your feelings and experience times when you are even controlled by those feelings. Either scenario may indicate a need for healing from a traumatic time in the past that has caused an unwanted behavior or reaction.

Some individuals have masked their feelings or denied them as a means of surviving painful events in their childhood. We have several in our classes who have emotional blocks of this nature. Often, vows made during trauma, such as "I will never be hurt again," cause people to shut off their feelings. The consequence, though, is they often don't have a capacity for enjoying good feelings either. As parents, they may have little tolerance for children who are strong feelers.

The comparison I like to share is that sometimes our feelings—or lack of feelings—can indicate that *there's something wrong "under the hood"*—similar to how your car might react if bad gas has been put in the tank. Instead of blaming others for how we feel, we need to understand it is our belief system that produces those feelings. In any given situation, we can have good or bad feelings; feelings that are rational or irrational. Either way, we are responsible for our own feelings because it's our belief system that creates them.

(4) Belief System (What Did You Believe?)

Your belief system is made up of a combination of sources: life experiences, opinions, perceptions, values, culture, memories, influence from peers or authority figures, teachings, self-talk, sources such as magazine articles, books, and media. All these sources influence or establish a belief system. That belief system is yours.

I was challenged myself in this area during my first few months in the mission field. I was working with people of different ages, cultures, and denominations. I soon realized, at the age of forty-five, that very few of my beliefs were my own. Rather, these beliefs had been implanted by others whom I did not question. I believed these people because of the authority they had in my life, and sometimes I believed what I did simply because I had no other reference to work from. Several of my beliefs began to be challenged. This was certainly an insecure and humbling time in my life.

Here is one example of what I'm talking about: We were visiting a church in Kealakekua, Hawaii, where the pastor wore a shiny silver suit. He reminded me of a television evangelist in this shiny silver suit, and I was immediately reminded of comments and opinions expressed by my mother whenever she saw a television evangelist on TV. I realized that I had a preconceived notion about this man I had never met.

I was determined to attend this church until I got to know the pastor. I enjoyed the worship, the people, and the teachings, and on the third week pastor Burton shared the story behind his suit. He said, "You know, some people might wonder why I wear a suit like this. Before I became a pastor," he explained, "I was a salesman for the Mercedes-Benz dealer here. When you sell cars for Mercedes-Benz, this is how you dress, and this is the only suit I have." Knowing the culture all around us where we were living—Hawaii—there are very few, if any, reasons a man would wear that suit.

I had to chuckle at myself. I also began to wonder how many other opinions and perceptions I owned that needed to be challenged. How many other beliefs in my belief system were grounded in prejudice or ignorance or were simply untrue?

The Total Emotion

Event – Behavior – Feeling – Belief

So now we know the typical sequence within an emotion triggered by a "hot button." When an *event* takes place, we usually don't process through it immediately, asking ourselves, "How do I feel about that?" Nor do we usually ask, "How do I want to react toward what just happened?" And most of us don't ask, "What is it I believe about what just happened?"

Instead, we typically react to a stimulus that has "triggered" us or pushed our "hot button" with a behavior we usually regret or must apologize for later. In the heat of the moment, we usually don't process how we feel or what we believe. I hear some think about those aspects later, and many times they use them to rationalize or excuse their own behavior: "I reacted that way because you made me feel so small when you said what you did and looked at me that way." In this scenario, they don't have to apologize for anything. They are making excuse for what they did.

In the rebuilding stage of our program, we would like to learn how to respond in a positive way, with a good attitude, with a renewed way of thinking. We would like to respond more appropriately, which means we try to set a *behavior goal*. If we have a behavior goal, of course, we need to set a *feeling goal*; but we can't change how we feel until we develop a new *belief*.

RENEWING YOUR MIND

> ...in reference to your former manner of life, you lay aside the old self, which is being corrupted in accordance with the lusts of deceit, <u>and that you be renewed in the spirit of your mind,</u> and put on the new self which, in the likeness of God, has been created in righteousness and holiness of the truth. (Ephesians 4:22–24, NASB)

> And do not be conformed to this world, but be transformed by the renewing of your mind, so that you may prove what the will of God is, that which is good and acceptable and perfect. (Romans 12:2, NASB)

COMMON DENOMINATORS

As people work through the LERC model, they often find there is a common denominator within their belief system associated with the various conflicts that arise in their life. After doing several of these exercises over some time, they often discover there is a common theme attached to their negative reaction. Some of the most typical common denominators are *trust, betrayal, control, injustice, rejection,* and *abandonment*.

Again, it seems as though God takes you around the same tree many times, only for the purpose of bringing you to a measure of healing in your own life. So identifying a common denominator can help you find the root of a conflict. For instance, if control is a common denominator, were there times in your life that were out of control? If it is injustice, what instances in your life did you witness or were you a victim of injustice? Is the phrase "It isn't fair" part of your vocabulary? If it is betrayal, identify times in your life when trust was broken. Whatever it is that you trace back to in your life, you will find in that place of wounding there is someone to forgive, something or someone to relinquish, a vow or a curse to break, or a false belief to renounce. God is calling you to renounce the lie and choose to believe the truth.

CORE BELIEF

I have either facilitated or led many classes and have done ministry with hundreds of hurting people. For most, their core belief as a result of their life experiences is "I'm unworthy ... of no value ... worthless ... unlovable ... a failure ... I don't matter."

Occasionally, during the first interview, I will ask, "What is your core belief about yourself?" and then, "Where do you think that comes from?"

CORE FEAR

This is a concept from author Gary Smalley in his book *DNA of Relationships*. There he shares a couple of points that are helpful when it comes to living in relationship. He calls this area of bondage our *core fear*. What I refer to as *common denominator* and what he calls *core fear* are essentially the same: fear of rejection, fear of control, fear of being out of control, fear of injustice, fear of abandonment, or fear of embarrassment. You can do an even deeper study of core fears by Googling *The Core Fear Test/Smalley Institute.*

We had a woman come for help who had been going to counselors since she was twelve. When I met her, she was in her forties. She suffered from chronic anxiety, which resulted in panic attacks. Of course, she was taking medication. When asked the cause of her present anxiety, she had an immediate response: It stemmed from a serious relationship she had with a man. They did not live in the same city, so they only saw each other on the weekends. If the boyfriend did not call for several days during the week, she would begin feeling anxious and eventually begin having panic attacks.

When asked about her childhood, she said that her childhood was normal. Further discussion revealed, her father traveled in his work and was only home on weekends. Also, her parents divorced when she was twelve. Following the divorce, she did not see or hear from her dad for several years. Abandonment! Rejection! I quickly responded, "Dear this is not a normal childhood". And her anxiety today is caused by what? The *fear of abandonment* and the *fear of rejection.*

EXPECTATIONS

This is another area Gary Smalley addresses so well in his book. He gives you an equation. What causes (equals) stress? When what you would like to see happen is very different from what actually happens, that equals stress. In other words, your expectations can cause more problems than you really have. Why? I have done ministry with adults who, at the age of forty and beyond, are still seeking approval from Mom and Dad. Every time the adult children visit their parents with the expectation or hope that this time Mom or Dad will treat them with respect or give them affirmation and acceptance, and this does not happen, the adult children are wounded all over again.

Expectations are also a part of the belief system. Expectations of who someone should be, or how they should behave, can easily be adopted as part of our belief system. What is the answer? Relinquishment: give up or lower your expectations, and accept them for who they are, instead of expecting them to be what you need. That may never happen.

In the chart shown later, the LERC (Life Event Revelation Chart), note that column B is where you may begin identifying, the common denominators, the core fears, and the core beliefs and expectations. You might also recognize that most of these can be traced back to vows, curses, judgments, and of course unforgiveness. You will identify these as areas for ministry.

Resolution

Here is one way this tool can be used to help resolve conflict. Ask the following questions: What happened? What did you do? How did you feel? What did you believe? Is there any time in your past where you felt the same way?

I have used this many times when working with couples and individuals to resolve a conflict, which usually involves a recurring event. When I ask the last question, "Is there any time in your past where you felt the same way?" the answer I often hear is "Yes, ever since I was eight-years-old and my mother told me …. Since then, what I believe and what I feel doesn't matter." That, my friends, is what I call a *core belief*. Is it truth? It is, to the one in bondage.

REDEMPTION

So knowing what you know about the redemptive process, what are the steps you can take to apply redemption to this core belief? Forgive Mother for what was said. Renounce the curse spoken over you. If the conflict is with a couple, I may ask the seeker to ask forgiveness for projecting the anger he has for his mother onto his wife, comparing her to his mother.

Most stubborn conflicts of life—that is, conflicts that cause us to overreact or become emotionally disabled—contain similar emotions and beliefs that directly correspond to or can be traced back to a hurtful event that happened in our family of origin, or at least to that period. The pain from that event causes us to download a negative program, so to speak, and without even needing to think about or consider how we feel when something similar happens, we immediately react to an event based on our life experience.

THE LERC MODEL

The LERC model, on the following page, is simply a tool used in conjunction with the Holy Spirit to identify false beliefs within our own personal belief system, specifically to repent or renounce (lay aside, cast off, turn away from) the false beliefs (lies) and replace them with the truth, God's Word.

Life Event Revelation Chart

A. Event	B. (Old Man) Belief System	C. Feelings	D. Behavior
What happened?	What did you believe? (Was what you believed truth?)	How did you feel?	What did you do? (Was your behavior out of balance with what happened?)
	Is there any time in your life when you believed or felt this way before?		
Was your perception of the event an objective view?	What would you need to believe to have different feelings?	How would you need to feel to have a good response?	In a similar event how would you like to respond?

CHAPTER 7

Rebuilding, Part II

REBUILDING OUR LIVES TO ALIGN WITH GOD'S PLUMB LINE

What has been shared in this book is essentially nothing more than basic Christianity. How to live it and how to apply it to our lives is what makes the difference. My desire is to help others learn principles that are foundational in life and essential to healthy relationships.

It is also my hope that these principles will not only continue to be practiced by the readers of this book, but will be passed on to their children so they might see the power of God in a tangible way working in their home. I hope our children will see God working in their lives "so they won't depart from it." In our opinion, the rebuilding component of the healing ministry is as important as the ministry itself. One of our teachers suggested that deliverance is 10 percent of the healing process. Walking out the healing is 90 percent. If we don't walk out our healing, some of us might spiral back to where we were.

We often spend weeks after ministry supplying tools for continued maintenance. It has been our experience that a cloud of deception has been lifted from a seeker's life in the first few weeks of ministry. The seeker is now able to see life more clearly than ever before. Because of this, seekers will begin receiving revelation in other areas where they would like to have freedom. As this happens, they need to have tools and principles they can apply to assist in continued healing.

Respond in the Opposite Spirit

One of the most important principles from Scripture to apply, is to respond in the opposite spirit. For example, if you have noticed that you have been critical or judgmental toward others, begin responding in the opposite spirit. When you catch yourself wanting to be critical or judgmental of another or others, look for ways you can encourage or compliment them. If you have been wallowing in self-pity, respond in the opposite spirit, and begin giving thanks for the many blessings in your life. It's all about being set free and keeping that freedom. Respond in the opposite spirit.

Common Challenges

Some common challenges are how we see ourselves, our negative self-talk, and the reality sometimes that we continue living with or relating to an individual we have had to forgive. Just because we have forgiven someone doesn't mean they are going to change. We will, however, have a greater tolerance toward the person, and we will have the ability to set healthier boundaries in that relationship. We have seen this happen with some seekers immediately after an initial ministry, which in itself is like a miracle. Others, however, may need additional help in learning how to set healthy boundaries. I suggest the *Boundaries* book or video series by Townsend and Cloud for seekers who need help in this area.

RECONCILIATION

Part of rebuilding is reconciliation. Being human means there are those we have offended or dishonored. For the sake of more freedom, many of us are compelled to seek the possibility of reconciliation not only with those we have offended but with those who have offended us as well. This attempt is not always successful the first time. Those who have tried this and not been successful had not prepared before attempting this next step toward complete freedom.

MY OFFENSE TOWARD OTHERS

The first time my wife and I went through a healing seminar, our initial response was turning to one another and declaring, "Oh my God, what have we done to our kids?" Our youngest was eighteen at the time. We soon thereafter made appointments with each child separately and went through the list of wrongs we had done. One by one, we described our mistaken behavior, told them how sorry we were, and asked for their forgiveness. We then asked each child to share the times one of us had hurt them, so we could deal with any other unresolved conflict as well.

Go to God, and ask who you may have hurt and how you have offended them. He will tell you. When you ask forgiveness, be direct: "I realize I hurt/offended you in this way. I am sorry for my actions. I was wrong. Will you forgive me?" (Be specific). Don't say, "If I have offended you …."

In each case, avoid making excuses or blaming someone (or something) else for your actions. If it is the first time you are discussing an offense, it may take the person some time to process the offense, and there may be some emotion involved. That is okay. Often family members may not be prepared for how to forgive effectively. They may try to pass off the offense as though it didn't matter and respond with "That's okay" or "That didn't bother me." When this happens, it seems the loop is never quite closed on the event. Please, for everyone's sake, process the offense with "Will you forgive me?" Then ask them if they forgive you. And they need to say, "Yes, I forgive you." If they can't forgive, you have done your part. You can go on.

Who Offended You

No one you have forgiven needs to be advised that you have forgiven them. You will not receive a merit badge for your mercy.

There is nothing to gain by approaching someone who abused you in the past and telling them you forgive them. This sometimes occurs by divine appointment only. Abusers may come asking forgiveness for what they did. Don't try to manipulate that. Let God do it.

There can, however, be an advantage in going to someone who hurt you if your reaction was ungodly. A positive outcome will only be accomplished, though, if you approach it the right way. When approaching someone who has wronged you, please go in humility, and repent of your inappropriate reaction to what happened. The son, for example, who rebelled and got into sex, drugs, and alcohol, cannot use what his father did to him as an excuse. Take responsibility for your own behavior, and go to your parents asking forgiveness for your inappropriate reaction. You will accomplish nothing and can even make things worse if you go to them and say, "I prayed and forgave you for all the horrible things you did to me as a kid."

It is quite common for one who offended or abused you as a child to believe they did nothing wrong. Your purpose in going to them is not to show them how wrong they were and how righteous you are. You are going in obedience to God for your own sin against them. Occasionally, they in turn will know that they played a part in your mistaken behavior and will also ask for forgiveness. Please don't approach them with this as a motive.

I do need to qualify that this procedure should not be attempted with a criminal action such as rape or incest. We have actually seen an instance where a woman thought she needed to tell the man who raped her that she had forgiven him. He simply laughed at her and raped her again.

Repentance

The beginning of change is repentance. Ask forgiveness, and accept accountability.

Trust

If trust has been broken, ask how you might be able to rebuild that trust.

Restitution

There may be a monetary value within some offenses. If so, you may need to make restitution and arrange a way to repay the debt.

GENERATIONAL SINS

We asked our children for forgiveness, and we prayed with them. We pointed out the generational sins we had identified so they could renounce them. We did not make excuses or try to blame someone else. Of course, this needs to be done at an age-appropriate time with the child.

GRIEVING

You may need to grieve a loss as part of the healing process. If you are still having regrets about areas you began to release in ministry, you may need time to grieve the loss you are experiencing. Some things we try to relinquish the right to, for example, may be difficult to release at first.

INAPPROPRIATE RESPONSES

Some mistaken ways to respond when asked for forgiveness include forgiving with conditions or saying; "That didn't bother me," "You always do that," or "You'll never change."

KEEP SHORT ACCOUNTS

When you recognize you've been hurt, go to the person and ask if you can talk about what happened. Often our own perception or a misunderstanding causes us to prejudge or add one offense onto another, until we have a difficult time knowing how it all started. Instead of dumping a ton of garbage on the other person, take it to the Lord or an accountability partner soon after an event happens.

The model my wife uses is that immediately she will go to God in prayer: "God, that hurt. I feel so rejected. I choose to forgive them, and I ask that You come and heal the hurt in my heart."

REJECTION

If you have been rejecting someone, go to them and ask forgiveness for your inappropriate behavior.

ATTITUDE

If you have had an attitude problem with someone, ask God to show you what the cause of the attitude is, and forgive them.

DO YOUR PART

Go in love. How others respond is their choice.

DON'T DENY

When someone hurts you, don't stuff it. Acknowledge the pain rather than denying it. Cry out to God if you must. "God, that hurt. I forgive them. Please come and heal this hurt in my heart."

GO TO THE CROSS DAILY

Consider the day, and ask the Lord what you need to release to Him. When negative thoughts come, renounce them, and begin claiming truth. This is key with passive-aggressive personalities. When you are hurt, forgive; when you catch yourself taking control again, repent and relinquish.

Confrontation

In most cases, your reason to confront someone should be that you care about them. Your motivation cannot be to show who is right or to get revenge. Confront for their benefit, not yours.

Expectations

Unmet expectations can be an ongoing hurt or offense if we allow them to be. We may have forgiven and be ready to move on, but the person we forgave may not have changed at all. This can cause a relapse if, say, we go home and expect Mom or Dad to treat us differently. This could be an unrealistic expectation and another opportunity to practice relinquishment.

Honor Your Father and Mother

Ask the Lord to identify instances of dishonor with spouses, parents, etc., and repent. (Fornication before marriage is dishonor toward spouse and parents in most cases.) In some homes, the best an adult child can do is honor the parent for giving birth.

I AM

If we have had a low estimation (low esteem) of ourselves, the "I AM" Scriptures can be a great help for this. When we have lies within our belief system, we can begin eliminating those lies by filling our mind and spirit with God's Word. (In this closing section, the Scripture quotations are all taken from the New Living Translation, either paraphrased or with pronouns modified to personalize them.)

I AM ...

God's child. For I have been born again. "My new life will last forever because it comes from the eternal, living word of God" (1 Peter 1:23).

Forgiven of all my sins and washed in the blood. "He is so rich in kindness and grace that He purchased my freedom with the blood of His Son and forgave my sins" (Ephesians 1:7; see also Hebrews 9:14; Colossians 1:14; and 1 John 1:9).

A New Person. "This means that anyone who belongs to Christ is a new person. The old life is gone; a new life has begun!" (2 Corinthians 5:17).

The temple of the Holy Spirit. I realize that my body is the temple of the Holy Spirit, who lives in me and was given to me by God (1 Corinthians 6:19).

Delivered from the power of darkness and brought into God's kingdom. "For He has rescued me from the kingdom of darkness and transferred me into the kingdom of His dear Son" (Colossians 1:13).

Redeemed from the curse of the Law. "I know that God paid a ransom to save me from the empty life I inherited from my ancestors. And it was not mere gold or silver. It was the precious blood of Christ, the sinless, spotless Lamb of God" (1 Peter 1:18–19).

Blessed. "So all who put their faith in Christ share the same blessing Abraham received because of his faith" (Galatians 3:9).

> You will experience all these blessings if you obey the Lord your God:
> Your towns and your fields will be blessed.
> Your children and your crops will be blessed. (Deuteronomy 28:2–4)

The head and not the tail. "If you listen to these commands of the Lord your God that I am giving you today, and if you carefully obey them, the Lord will make you the head and not the tail, and you will always be on top and never at the bottom" (Deuteronomy 28:13).

Holy and without fault before Him. "Even before He made the world, God loved me and chose me in Christ to be holy and without fault in His eyes" (Ephesians 1:4; see also 1 Peter 1:16.

God's chosen. "Since God chose you to be the holy people He loves, you must clothe yourselves with tenderhearted mercy, kindness, humility, gentleness, and patience" (Colossians 3:12; see also Romans 8:33).

Strong to the end. "He will keep me strong to the end so that I will be free from all blame on the day when our Lord Jesus Christ returns" (1 Corinthians 1:–8).

Brought near by the blood of Christ. "But now I have been united with Christ Jesus. Once I was far away from God, but now I have been brought near to Him through the blood of Christ" (Ephesians 2:13).

Set free. "Jesus said to the people who believed in Him, 'You are truly My disciples if you remain faithful to My teachings. And you will know the truth, and the truth will set you free'" (John 8:31–32).

Dead to sin. "He personally carried my sins in His body on the cross so that I can be dead to sin and live for what is right. By His wounds I am healed" (1 Peter 2:24).

A joint heir with Christ. "And since I am His child, I am His heir. In fact, together with Christ I am an heir of God's glory. But if I am to share His glory, I must also share His suffering" (Romans 8:17).

Sealed with the Holy Spirit of promise. "And now you Gentiles have also heard the truth, the Good News that God saves you. And when you believed in Christ, He identified you as His own by giving you the Holy Spirit, whom He promised long ago" (Ephesians 1:13).

Crucified with Christ. "My old self has been crucified with Christ. It is no longer I who live, but Christ lives in me. So I live in this earthly body by trusting in the Son of God, who loved me and gave Himself for me" (Galatians 2:20).

Alive with Christ. "But God is so rich in mercy, and He loved me so much, that even though I was dead because of my sins, He gave me life when He raised Christ from the dead" (Ephesians 2:4–5).

Free from condemnation. "So now there is no condemnation for those who belong to Christ Jesus" (Romans 8:1).

In God's family and the evil one cannot reach me. "I know that God's child does not make a practice of sinning, for God's Son holds me securely, and the evil one cannot touch me" (1 John 5:18).

Made right with God. "For God made Christ, who never sinned, to be the offering for my sin, so that I could be made right with God through Christ" (2 Corinthians 5:21).

Sharing His divine nature. "And because of His glory and excellence, He has given me great and precious promises. These are the promises that enable me to share His divine nature and escape the world's corruption caused by human desires" (2 Peter 1:4).

God's choice possession out of all creation. "He chose to give birth to me by giving me His true word. And I, out of all creation, became His prized possession" (James 1:18).

God's masterpiece, created in Christ Jesus for good works. "For I am God's masterpiece. He has created me anew in Christ Jesus, so I can do the good things He planned for me long ago" (Ephesians 2:10).

Being changed into His image. "So all of us who have had that veil removed can see and reflect the glory of the Lord. And the

Lord—who is the Spirit—makes us more and more like Him as we are changed into His glorious image" (2 Corinthians 3:18; see also Philippians 1:6).

Raised up with Christ and seated in heavenly places. "For He raised me from the dead along with Christ and seated me with Him in the heavenly realms because I am united with Christ Jesus" (Ephesians 2:6; see also Colossians 2:12).

I Have ...

Received an inheritance. "Furthermore, because I am united with Christ, I have received an inheritance from God, for He chose me in advance, and He makes everything work out according to His plan" (Ephesians 1:11).

The peace of God, which is beyond understanding. "Then I will experience God's peace, which exceeds anything I can understand. His peace will guard my heart and mind as I live in Christ Jesus" (Philippians 4:7).

Received power ... the power of the Holy Spirit; power to lay hands on the sick and see them recover, power to cast out demons, power over all the power of the enemy, and nothing shall by any means hurt me (Mark 16:17–18).

I Live …

By the Spirit of life. "And because I belong to Him, the power of the life-giving Spirit has freed me from the power of sin that leads to death" (Romans 8:2).

In Christ. "For I can do everything through Christ, who gives me strength" (Philippians 4:13).

I Am Created …

Name:_____

I am created in God's image. "Then God said, 'Let us make human beings in our image, to be like us. They will reign over the fish in the sea, the birds in the sky, the livestock, all the wild animals on the earth, and the small animals that scurry along the ground.' So God created human beings in His own image. In the image of God He created them; male and female He created them" (Genesis 1:26–27).

God loves me unconditionally for who I am. "But God showed His great love for me by sending Christ to die for me while I was still a sinner" (Romans 5:8).

I am justified. "Therefore, since I have been made right in God's sight by faith, I have peace with God because of what Jesus Christ my Lord has done for me" (Romans 5:1).

I am a child of God. I belong to God's family and household. "So now we Gentiles are no longer strangers and foreigners. We are citizens along with all of God's holy people. We are members of God's family. Together, we are His house, built on the foundation of the apostles and the prophets. And the cornerstone is Christ Jesus Himself" (Ephesians 2:19–20).

I am a child of God, adopted into His eternal family. "God decided in advance to adopt me into His own family by bringing me to himself through Jesus Christ. This is what He wanted to do, and it gave Him great pleasure" (Ephesians 1:5).

Lord, I believe You.

Signed: _____

The Cross

What Jesus Did for Me

* *He took my **punishment** that I might be forgiven.* "Yet it was our weaknesses He carried; it was our sorrows that weighed Him down. And we thought His troubles were a punishment from God, a punishment for His own sins! But He was pierced for our rebellion, crushed for our sins. He was beaten so we could be whole. He was whipped so we could be healed" (Isaiah 53:4–5).
* *He was **wounded** that I might be **healed*** (Isaiah 53:5).

* *He was made **sin** with my sinfulness that I might be made **righteous** with His righteousness.* "But it was the Lord's good plan to crush Him and cause Him grief. Yet when His life is made an offering for sin, He will have many descendants. He will enjoy a long life, and the Lord's good plan will prosper in His hands. When He sees all that is accomplished by His anguish, He will be satisfied. And because of His experience, my righteous servant will make it possible for many to be counted righteous, for He will bear all their sins" (Isaiah 53:10–11).

* *He tasted **death** for me that I might share His **life**.* "What we do see is Jesus, who was given a position 'a little lower than the angels'; and because He suffered death for us, He is now 'crowned with glory and honor.' Yes, by God's grace, Jesus tasted death for everyone" (Hebrews 2:9).

* *He was made a **curse** for me that I might receive a **blessing**.* "But Christ has rescued me from the curse pronounced by the law. When He was hung on the Cross, He took upon himself the curse for my wrongdoing. For it is written in the Scriptures, 'Cursed is everyone who is hung on a tree.' Through Christ Jesus, God has blessed the Gentiles with the same blessing He promised to Abraham, so that I who am a believer might receive the promised Holy Spirit through faith" (Galatians 3:13–14).

* *He endured **poverty** that I might share His **abundance**.* "I know the generous grace of my Lord Jesus Christ. Though He was rich, yet for my sake He became poor, so that by His poverty He could make me rich" (2 Corinthians 8:9).

* *My **old self** was put to death that my **new self** might come to life in me.* "I know that my old sinful self was crucified with Christ

so that sin might lose its power in my life. I am no longer a slave to sin. For when I died with Christ I was set free from the power of sin. And since I died with Christ, I know I will also live with Him" (Romans 6:6–8).

"The Dirty Dozen"

Beliefs Guaranteed to Make Your Life Miserable

1. I must be approved of and loved by all the significant others in my life.
2. Everyone should think or believe the way I do.
3. I should never make mistakes. I should never fail. I should be perfect.
4. I should never let anyone down (especially those I love).
5. My life must be conflict-free (especially with those closest to me).
6. I need to be accepted by others at all costs.
7. My life should always be happy.
8. Everyone needs to understand me.
9. Everyone needs to agree with me (especially those who love me).
10. I need to perform well to be loved and accepted.
11. No one may dislike (or hate) me.
12. I can't change the way I am.

Names of God

Prayer of Adoration – "Hallowed Be Thy Name"
Taken from *Prayers That Avail Much*,
published by Word Ministries, Inc.

Our Father, which art in heaven, hallowed be Thy name.

Bless the Lord, O my soul; and all that is within me, bless Your holy name. I adore You and make known to You my adoration and love this day.

I bless Your name, Elohim, the Creator of heaven and earth, who was in the beginning. It is You who made me, and You have crowned me with glory and honor. You are the God of might and strength. Hallowed be Thy name!

I bless Your name, El-Shaddai, the God Almighty of blessings. You are the Breasted One who nourishes and supplies. You are All-Bountiful and All-Sufficient. Hallowed be Thy name!

I bless Your name, Adonai, my Lord and my Master. You are Jehovah—the Completely Self-Existing One, always present, revealed in Jesus, who is the same yesterday, today, and forever. Hallowed be Thy name!

I bless Your name, Jehovah-Jireh, the One who sees my needs and provides for them. Hallowed be Thy name!

I bless Your name, Jehovah-Rapha, my Healer and the One who makes bitter experiences sweet. You sent Your Word and healed me. You forgave all my iniquities, and You healed all my diseases. Hallowed be Thy name!

I bless Your name, Jehovah-M'Kaddesh, the Lord my Sanctifier. You have set me apart for Yourself. Hallowed be Thy name!

I bless Your name, Jehovah-Nissi, You are my Victory, my Banner, and my Standard. Your banner over me is love. When the enemy shall come in like a flood, You will lift up a standard against him. Hallowed be Thy name!

Jehovah-Shalom, I bless Your name. You are my Peace—the peace which transcends all understanding; which garrisons and mounts guard over my heart and mind in Christ Jesus. Hallowed be Thy name!

I bless Your name, Jehovah-Tsidkenu, my Righteousness. Thank You for becoming sin for me that I might become the righteousness of God in Christ Jesus. Hallowed be Thy name!

I bless Your name, Jehovah-Rohi, You are my Shepherd, and I shall not want for any good or beneficial thing. Hallowed be Thy name!

Hallelujah to Jehovah-Shammah, who will never leave or forsake me. You are always there. I take comfort and am encouraged and confidently and boldly say, "The Lord is my Helper. I will not be seized with alarm; I will not fear or dread or be terrified. What can man do to me?" Hallowed be Thy name!

I worship and adore You, El-Elyon, the Most High God who is the First Cause of everything, the Possessor of the heavens and earth. You are the everlasting God, the Great God, the Living God, the Merciful God, the Faithful God, and the Mighty God. You are Truth, Justice, Righteousness, and Perfection. You are El-Elyon—the highest sovereign of the heavens and the earth. Hallowed be Thy name!

Father, You have exalted above all else Your name and Your Word, and You have magnified Your Word. The Word was made flesh and dwelt among us, and His name is Jesus! Hallowed be Thy name!

Resources for Rebuilding

- *Living in the Freedom of the Spirit* by Tom Marshall
    A must for any Christian in search of practical application of biblical principles.
- *Right Relationships* by Tom Marshall
    A biblical foundation for building or mending relationships.
- *Codependent No More* by Melody Beattie
    Adult Children of Alcoholics and other dysfunctional families.
- *Telling Yourself the Truth* by William Backus
    Establishing healthy belief systems.
- *Victory Over the Darkness* by Neil Anderson
    Establish healthy belief systems and break spiritual bondages.
- *Boundaries* by Henry Cloud and John Townsend
    Getting others to recognize and respect my boundaries.
- *The Peace and Power of Knowing god's Name* by Kay Arthur
    The truth about God's Father heart and true character.
- *Healing for Damaged Emotions* by David Seamonds
    Emotional healing.
- *The Wounded Heart* by David Allender
    Healing for sexual abuse.
- *Released from Shame* by Sandra Wilson
    Healing for sexual abuse, adult children of alcoholics, and others.

- *Your Wife Was Sexually Abused* by John Courtright and Sid Rogers
    Good support for the spouse.
- *Sexual Healing* by David Foster
    Sexual addictions, homosexuality, pornography, and masturbation.
- *The Anger Work Book* by Les Carter and Frank Minirth
    Proper release of anger. Self-control (recommended to do this with a helper for ministry).
- *Blessing or Curse* by Derik Prince
    Recognize the power of negative words, demonic strongholds, and other spiritual bondages; recommended that couples read and pray through this together).
- *Search for Significance* by Robert McGee
    A great workbook for identifying specific areas of healing, including how to look at the offenses from all angles. Extremely deep.
- *The Father Heart of God* by Floyd McClung
    Identify why we have difficulty coming to the revelation of God as our Father.
- *Why You Do the Things You Do* by Tim Clinton
    Identifying the causes of relationship breakdown and conflict.
- *From Shame to Peace* by Teo Van der Weele
    Learning the culture of the abused.
- *Walls of the Heart* by Dr. Bruce Thompson
    The divine plumb line in book form.
- *The Blessing* by John Trent
    All about the Father's blessing.
- *The Snoodles Tale* by Veggie Tales
    Video.

Made in the USA
Monee, IL
24 February 2022